Unwin Education Books

POSITIVE TEACHING

Unwin Education Books

Education Since 1800 IVOR MORRISH
Physical Education for Teaching BARBARA CHURCHER
Organising and Integrating the First School Day JOY TAYLOR
The Philosophy of Education: An Introduction HARRY SCHOFIELD
Assessment and Testing: An Introduction HARRY SCHOFIELD
Education: Its Nature and Purpose M. V. C. JEFFREYS
Learning in the Primary School KENNETH HASLAM
The Sociology of Education: An Introduction IVOR MORRISH
Developing a Curriculum AUDREY and HOWARD NICHOLLS
Teacher Education and Cultural Change H. DUDLEY PLUNKETT and
  JAMES LYNCH
Reading and Writing in the First School JOY TAYLOR
Approaches to Drama DAVID A. MALE
Aspects of Learning BRIAN O'CONNELL
Focus on Meaning JOAN TOUGH
Moral Education WILLIAM KAY
Concepts in Primary Education JOHN E. SADLER
Moral Philosophy for Education ROBIN BARROW
Principle of Classroom Learning and Perception RICHARD J. MUELLER
Education and the Community ERIC MIDWINTER
Creative Teaching AUDREY and HOWARD NICHOLLS
The Preachers of Culture MARGARET MATHIESON
Mental Handicap: An Introduction DAVID EDEN
Aspects of Educational Change IVOR MORRISH
Beyond Initial Reading JOHN POTTS
The Foundations of Maths in the Infant School JOY TAYLOR
Common Sense and the Curriculum ROBIN BARROW
The Second 'R' WILLIAM HARPIN
The Diploma Disease RONALD DORE
The Development of Meaning JOAN TOUGH
The Place of Commonsense in Educational Thought LIONEL ELVIN
Language in Teaching and Learning HAZEL FRANCIS
Patterns of Education in the British Isles NIGEL GRANT and ROBERT BELL
Philosophical Foundations for the Curriculum ALLEN BRENT
World Faiths in Education W. OWEN COLE
Classroom Language: What Sort? JILL RICHARDS
Philosophy and Human Movement DAVID BEST
Secondary Schools and the Welfare Network DAPHNE JOHNSON et al.
Educating Adolescent Girls E. M. CHANDLER
Classroom Observation of Primary School Children RICHARD W. MILLS
Essays on Educators R. S. PETERS
Comparative Education: Some Considerations of Method BRIAN HOLMES
Education and the Individual BRENDA COHEN
Moral Development and Moral Education R. S. PETERS
In-Service Education within the School ROLAND W. MORANT
Learning to Read HAZEL FRANCIS
Children and Schooling PHILIP GAMMAGE
Relating to Learning PETER KUTNICK
The Foundations of Morality JOEL J. KUPPERMAN
Child Management in the Primary School TESSA ROBERTS
Managing Educational Innovations AUDREY NICHOLLS
Paradigms and Language Games DAVID STENHOUSE
The Libertarians and Education MICHAEL P. SMITH
Philosophy and Educational Foundations ALLEN BRENT

Positive Teaching
The Behavioural
Approach

KEVIN WHELDALL and FRANK MERRETT

Centre for Child Study, Department of Educational Psychology,
University of Birmingham

London
GEORGE ALLEN & UNWIN
Boston   Sydney

George Allen & Unwin (Publishers) Ltd,
40 Museum Street, London WC1A 1LU, UK

George Allen & Unwin (Publishers) Ltd,
Park Lane, Hemel Hempstead, Herts HP2 4TE, UK

Allen & Unwin, Inc.,
9 Winchester Terrace, Winchester, Mass. 01890, USA

George Allen & Unwin Australia Pty Ltd,
8 Napier Street, North Sydney, NSW 2060, Australia

First published in 1984

British Library Cataloguing in Publication Data

Wheldall, Kevin
  Positive teaching.
1. Classroom management 2. Educational
psychology
I. Title II. Merrett, Frank
371.1'024   LB3013
ISBN-04-370150-7
ISBN 0-04-370151-5 Pbk

Library of Congress Cataloging in Publication Data

Wheldall, Kevin.
  The behavioural approach.
Bibliography: p.
Includes index.
1. Classroom management—Addresses, essays, lectures.
2. Teaching—Addresses, essays, lectures. 3. Behavior
modification—Addresses, essays, lectures. 4. Individualized
instruction—Addresses, essays, lectures. 5. Group work in
education—Addresses, essays, lectures.
I. Merrett, Frank.   II. Title.
LB3013.W47   1984   371.1'024   84-6220
ISBN 0-04-370150-7
ISBN 0-04-370151-5 (pbk.)

Set in 10 on 11 Times by Preface Ltd, Salisbury
and printed in Great Britain
by Biddles Ltd, Guildford, Surrey

Reward it is, that makes us good or bad.

(Herrick, 1591–1674, *Hesperides*)

'Tis Education forms the common Mind,
Just as the Twig is bent, the Tree's inclined.

(Pope, 1688–1744, *Moral Essays*)

Contents

Preface

This book is designed for teachers and student teachers who want to improve their teaching performance in the classroom or, in other words, who want to become more effective teachers. The use of corporal punishment is finally on the decline in British schools and this has been accompanied by a renewed interest in seeking out alternative, more positive methods of working with children. Throughout this book we are arguing the case for a consistent and positive approach in our relationships with children in school. Moreover, and this is rare in education, the *behavioural* approach suggested here has been carefully researched and scientifically evaluated. The methods we advocate are all firmly based on behavioural principles and have all been carefully and rigorously tried and tested by the authors in their work with teachers. We have shown how simple and straightforward interventions by teachers can bring about dramatic results in terms of improved classroom atmosphere and the quantity and quality of work produced. Moreover, these methods have been shown to yield a more satisfying and rewarding classroom experience for teachers and children. In other words, and less pompously, the behavioural approach to teaching is more fun for all concerned.

The scope of this book is deliberately limited. It is not meant to serve as an encyclopaedic review of all aspects of teaching. Curriculum content and development are covered exhaustively in numerous texts but little attention is ever given to how teachers might *behave* in classrooms in order to bring about suitable conditions for learning to take place effectively and efficiently. Teachers have traditionally been concerned with children's social as well as their academic behaviours, usually in terms of suppressing the former to encourage the latter. In this book we are concerned almost solely with problems of social behaviour: with encouraging children to behave socially in ways which will maximise their opportunities for learning appropriate academic skills and information.

There have been other introductory texts advocating

behavioural approaches, some of them excellent, but they have
either not been particularly designed for teachers or have had a
very wide scope (and hence have been very long!) and have almost
invariably been North American in origin. It seems obvious to us
that the management of social behaviour in the classroom is a
sufficiently important and worrying topic to warrant an exhaustive
treatment. Whereas parents, social workers and others might also
have difficulties in this area, teachers experience a highly specific
set of problem behaviours, not least because they are often dealing
with groups of children as well as individuals. We believe that this
book is the first *British* text aimed exclusively at *teachers* which
deals solely with the *management of social behaviour* in schools.
Our experience is that North American texts, however good, tend
to travel badly in so far as British teachers find it difficult to relate
their experience to the examples given. British teachers are,
perhaps rightly, wary of directly importing techniques originally
demonstrated in the United States since there are many cultural
differences   and   the   education   systems   are   dissimilar.
Recommendations to use transistor radios and Hallowe'en outfits
as rewards for good behaviour will ring hollow in the ears of
British teachers struggling to provide the bare essentials, such as
paper and pencils, on a meagre budget. Our aim is to translate the
American experience into a British context and to demonstrate
that expensive rewards and equipment are an unnecessary luxury
and may, in fact, be counter-productive. In the second part of this
book we present a series of demonstration studies carried out by
British teachers in their own schools and classrooms, under the
guidance of the authors. All of these studies were simple to set up,
used inexpensive materials already to hand and could be carried
through without any extra help.

Before concluding this preface we would like to make three
small but pertinent points. First, we have deliberately referred to
teachers of both sexes throughout the book, to avoid sexist
assumptions, but we have attempted, where possible, to refer to
the child as being of the opposite sex to the teacher, for the sake of
clarity. Secondly, in order to make some points concisely we found
it helpful to include some 'jargon' (technical words). We have kept
these to what we believe to be the minimum. The first time each
technical word is used it is italicised for emphasis and is followed
by some explanation of its meaning. Knowledge of these key
technical terms will also make it easier for the interested reader
when consulting other texts and articles. Thirdly, our behavioural

approach to learning convinces us that human beings learn best when, in addition to reading about problems, they respond to them actively. Consequently, we have included a number of exercises in each chapter which are designed to encourage active responding on your part. We would urge you to attempt these exercises systematically in order to get the best out of the book. Many of the questions have no 'right' answers but suggestions regarding possible solutions for all the exercises have been grouped together at the back of the book.

Finally we would like to thank the various individuals who have helped us in the writing and researching of this book. These include: teachers and children, too numerous to mention, who have tolerated our presence in their classrooms; our students, Bob Austin, Kate Bevan, Margaret Biggs, Dot Blundell, Pat Elliot, John Hackett, Audrey Little, Linda McGrath, Valerie McPhee, Marian Morris, Maggie Moore, Yin Yuk Ng, Gordon O'Connell, Lorraine Petersen, Brian Pickthorne, Lesley Richards, Jean Shiner, Janet Steed, Pamela Vaughan, Elaine Warner and Dorrie Wheldall, who have attempted our suggestions and read earlier drafts of this book; Nick Beard for allowing us to use a modified version of his scale in the introduction; Margaret Pallant for producing beautiful, successive drafts from a seemingly ever-changing and increasingly indecipherable manuscript; Susan Colmar, Audree Hay, Robert Lambourne and Stan Kesterton for their detailed criticisms and many helpful suggestions; and Allan Russell for encouraging us to avoid using what he calls 'half-crown words'. Any remaining errors or infelicities of style remain, of course, our responsibility alone. We sincerely hope that this book will help you to improve your teaching.

KEVIN WHELDALL and FRANK MERRETT
1984

Part One

The Behavioural Approach to Teaching

Chapter 1

Introduction: Setting the Scenes

Teaching is an exhausting business; not physically but mentally. The exhaustion felt by teachers at the end of the day, and more especially at the end of the term, is the result of having to make snap decisions in a great variety of situations, which are constantly changing. In most of these situations teachers are, in addition, responsible for the well-being and academic progress of their charges. For the beginner, this is daunting as well as exhausting. By degrees teachers learn to cope by 'learning on the job' but, once out of their probationary year, they do this on their own by rule of thumb, seldom finding the time or the opportunity to stand back and consider what is happening to their behaviour or that of their classes.

Advances in educational psychology have helped to make life easier for teachers in some respects. Knowledge of the intellectual, social and emotional development of children, for example, provides teachers with an invaluable framework upon which to build a school curriculum. A knowledge of ages and stages helps teachers to decide *when* to teach *what*. Similarly, cognitive psychologists have passed on their discoveries about how information is received, processed and stored, thereby providing useful information about *how* material might ideally be presented to maximise learning. Psychology has also had a great influence on the methods of evaluating children's progress so that more objective measures are now possible. In all of these areas educational psychology has helped to make the difficult lot of the teacher a little easier.

But in spite of all this, teaching is still a complex business. Very little time is spent during most college courses in actually dealing with everyday, practical problems occurring in classrooms. There is little emphasis on teaching teachers the classroom management skills which it is necessary to learn in order to become really effective. Moreover, it is very rare that an all-embracing theoretical model of teaching is explicitly presented which enables the teacher to understand what is happening in classrooms. Ideally, such a model would have implications for what teachers should do; it should have an accompanying methodology for approaching and analysing problems and a technology for solving them. In this book we are presenting what we believe to be the best teaching model so far discovered which encompasses a sound theoretical basis, a methodology and a technology, and which, if seriously considered and practised, can yield more effective teaching and a more rewarding teaching experience. We call this model *positive teaching* or the behavioural approach to teaching.

The day-to-day problems classroom teachers face are probably all too vivid to you, but let us now follow a young teacher, Jan, and look in on some of her encounters during a typical day at school. Many teachers will doubtless feel great empathy with Jan and her attempts to come to terms with the diverse, and apparently unrelated, conceptual difficulties she experiences. The behavioural approach to teaching will provide the model to show how Jan's difficulties can be understood within a common framework. We will return to this in Chapter 2.

SCENE 1

Jan sipped moodily at her cup of coffee, staring vacantly out of the staffroom window. Her gloomy thoughts as to whether she would ever gain a scale two post were violently interrupted when a 9-year-old Lancaster bomber swept over the horizon and across the playground. Machine guns blazed as Gary from the third year mercilessly gunned down his classmates, arms outstretched winging his way back across the school yard in solitary play. As she watched, the plane faltered and lurched badly, as Gary's feet skidded on the loose gravel, and came to an undignified end in a crumpled heap. From where she stood, Jan could see clearly that apart from falling on his well-padded bottom, the only injury he had sustained was a mild case of wounded pride and she was amazed to see the boy begin to howl. Fists furiously rubbing his eyes, he rushed over to Eileen who was on playground duty nearby. Jan continued to watch as Eileen knelt to comfort the sobbing child, wiping his eyes with a tissue until she managed to raise a smile from him. With a quick wave of thanks, Gary then resumed his previous posture and made a perfect take-off into the slate grey sky.

'He's a funny lad, isn't he, that Gary Summers? He seems to cry at the slightest thing. Proper mardy, as we used to say in Derby. It's not what you'd expect from a great, strapping lad like Gary.'

Jan had not noticed that her friend Hilary was standing behind her. 'Yes', she replied thoughtfully, 'I've noticed that too.'

'I'll tell you one thing, though', continued Hilary. 'I was standing just where you are the other week and watched him playing with some of the older boys in your top class. They were playing at pirates and one of them accidentally caught Gary with the back of his hand. He started to cry, of course, but the older lads just laughed in disbelief and ran off, and left him to it.'

As the two friends talked, Gary landed his Lancaster in the midst of the group of older boys Hilary had just mentioned and joined in their game of commandos. The sound of battle cries filtered through the staffroom window as a play punch from one of the top-class commandos connected and Gary was sent reeling against the wall.

'Gosh, sorry Gary, I didn't mean it', said the commando.

'S'all right', said Gary looking round and picking himself up. 'Didn't 'urt.'

'Coo – bet it did', responded the commando in genuine admiration. 'Come on, I'll be the German this time.'

Inside the staffroom the two teachers watched in amazement.

'Well I'll be damned!' said Hilary. 'Aren't kids funny.'

Jan nodded in silent agreement. What was it that made kids like Gary behave in such an unpredictable way?

SCENE 2

Sarah was a 10-year-old in Jan's class. She was a likeable girl but painfully slow, especially in maths lessons. Sarah would just be starting the second problem by the time most of the others had finished their first work-card and had gone on to another.

'Come on, Sarah', Jan would frequently say, breezily, to hide her concern. 'A snail could work quicker than that.' And the class would titter whilst Sarah smiled sleepily.

Jan had spoken to Sarah's parents who had assured her that she always went to bed by 9.00 and usually slept soundly until 7.30 the next day. 'Perhaps she's got a block about maths', Hilary had volunteered. 'I'm like that too. I go to pieces when I see numbers. Thank goodness I teach reception!'

'What makes you think that?' Jan had asked.

'Well, she can't do her sums, can she?' Hilary had replied airily. 'It stands to reason that she must have a block about it. You know, number blindness; like word blindness, dyslexia. I bet Colin, your psychologist friend, has got a posh word for it.'

'But she *can* do the work', Jan had persisted, ignoring the jibe. 'The few sums she does do she invariably gets right. It's just that she hardly does any!'

'Well, maybe she's just a bit slow then, a bit backward perhaps', Hilary had said, unwilling to give up. 'There must be some reason.'

'Maybe', Jan had replied. 'But that doesn't tell me what to do to help her.'

Later on that morning after break, Jan popped in to see Eileen in her adjoining third-year class in order to ask her advice about Sarah. Jan, who had taught the same class when they were in their second year the year before, looked out warily for her 'bad lads', a trio of cheerful trouble-makers who had continually disrupted her lessons. She was amazed to hear Eileen saying to one of them, 'That's tremendous Tommy, you're really working well today', and there was Tommy, and the other two, working away like beavers.

'Well, my "bad lads" have certainly grown up a bit since last year', whispered Jan, when she caught Eileen's attention.

'Oh, they're all smashing kids', laughed Eileen. 'We really have a good time and yet they're so willing to work hard when I ask them to. I guess different classes react differently to different teachers. Oh, excuse me a moment.' And with that she turned back to her class. 'Well done, class 3, I could have heard a pin drop while I was talking to Miss Hastings. That's what I like to see. I think we'll do some drama this afternoon.' The class murmured delightedly and then quickly went back to their work. Eileen turned back to Jan and looked at her expectantly.

'Oh, I was just going to ask your advice about Sarah', said Jan lamely, 'but it will keep till lunch-time. I must get back to my class.'

As she was returning to her pupils, she felt helpless. It seemed to her that some of her colleagues just had it made – they were *born* teachers. Entering her own classroom again, she put these thoughts aside and heard herself saying, 'Sit down Anthony! How many times do I have to tell you. . .'

SCENE 3

That afternoon Jan had an appointment to visit the nearby comprehensive school to which most of her class would be moving after the summer holidays. It was funny to think of her kids going on to secondary school – they seemed so young still. She had been invited to sit in on a first-year maths class for the first part of the afternoon, and made her way to room M45, pausing to peer through the half-glazed door before going in to introduce herself to the teacher in charge. The general hubbub finally died as the maths teacher shouted to make himself heard.

'OK. Just shut up and get your homework books out. Right, pass them forward. Adams, you're a twit! Sit down and stop messing about. Always the clown, aren't you, eh?'

'Yes sir.'

Muted mirth bubbled around the room.

'. . . twenty-eight, twenty-nine, thirty. Hang on, there should be thirty-one. OK. Who's not handed in their homework? Come on, own up. I *can* count, you know, even if you illiterate, innumerate morons can't. Shut up! That's not funny! Now, who's not handed it in. Come on, I can easily find out.'

Sniggering stares, ruler poking and downcast eyes identified Adams as the culprit.

'So it's our friend Adams again. I should have guessed, shouldn't I?'

'Yes sir.'

'And might we be privileged to hear why not, Adams? Too busy working on extrapolations from Einstein's theory of relativity, were we?'

Sycophantic tittering rose from the class.

'Shut up! I'm talking to our mathematical genius friend Adams, who's too brilliant to bother with homework. Is that right, Adams?'

'No sir.'

'Well, come on laddie, why didn't you do the work I set you then? Come on, I'm waiting!'

'Lost me pen sir.'

Smiles spread across the room like an infectious disease.

'Lost your pen? Stop smirking you lot! Lost your pen? You are a twit Adams! What are you?'

'A twit sir . . . and . . . and a moron sir.'

The giggles began at the back and swept, like a wave, over the rows of desks.

'You are a FOOL, Adams! You could have borrowed a pen. You just didn't do it because you're a lazy, idle, good-for-nothing little . . . words fail me. SHUT UP YOU LOT! You continually have to kick against the pricks, don't you Adams? That's not FUNNY! You've got minds like sewers.'

The class are helpless by now – this is even better than Basil Fawlty.

'You were too busy, Adams. Is that it? Too busy watching Starsky and Hutch, perhaps?'

'It's not on on Tuesday sir.'

Someone on the back row cheered whilst others pointed to the clock which indicated that at least ten minutes of the lesson had already been wasted.

'Shut up! Or too busy reading comics, eh? Tell me, Adams, does Desperate Dan still eat cow pies? I'm sure you must be an expert on this monumental figure of English literature.'

'Yes sir, I mean no sir . . . I mean, yes he does sir.'

'Shut up you lot! I'm sick and tired of your tittering. That's NOT funny! And you Adams are in detention again. That's the third night this week and it's only Wednesday. You know something Adams? Sometimes I don't think you know the meaning of the word punishment.'

Jan watched and listened horrified and then walked away. She had heard enough. She remembered how she had seen Eileen coping with her 'bad lads' earlier and thought to herself, 'There must be better ways of handling kids like these'.

SCENE 4

Returning home on the suburban line train that evening, Jan tried to piece together her conflicting impressions of a confusing day, whilst trying to read the *Times Educational Supplement* at the same time. She was hindered in both of these activities by the voluble presence of a family occupying a set of seats nearby.

The young parents sat sullenly amidst their brood of three little girls aged from about 18 months to 4 years. He stared fixedly at the sports pages of his newspaper whilst she puffed determinedly at a cigarette, showering ash and smoke over the toddler on her lap. Jan could not help watching and overhearing what followed.

'Moo-cow', said the middle girl, Tracey-Diane, looking out at the passing fields.

'And sheep', said the eldest, Sharon.

Silence from both parents.

'Look', continued Sharon. 'Cows an' sheep . . . look Mum . . . Mum, look cows an' sheep . . . Mum' (louder), 'Mum, look!' (louder). No response from either parent. 'Mum, look', continued the little girl, unwilling to give up. 'MUM, LOOK', she yelled this time, and shook her mother's arm.

'Shut yer face, Sharon, or I'll give you cows an' sheep', hissed her mother, her eyes narrowing. 'Dave, you tell 'er . . . Dave, I said you tell 'er . . . DAVE!'

'What's up?' said Dave. 'Shurrup Sharon, I'm fed up of talking to you.'

Jan vaguely recollected something her tutor at college had said about Bernstein, a sociologist, as she watched the same routine repeat itself several times more. The topic changed, but the pattern of increasingly loud demands from the child and the eventual response from the parents remained almost identical. Threats and angry shakings seemed to have no effect on the little girl, and her continual demands for attention remained unanswered until she reached an unspecified threshold of loudness.

As she listened to the fifth action replay of this 'mother–child interaction' Jan felt as if she had found another piece of her jigsaw puzzle, but did not know how it fitted in. . . .

SCENE 5

'It's good to see you again', said Colin smiling across the restaurant table at her, later that evening. 'You look great!'

'I don't feel it', admitted Jan. 'I've had a really frustrating day. That's why I called you in fact – I'm in need of "psychological" advice. No, stop laughing, I'm not cracking up! It's about the kids in my school. I really like kids, you know. I wouldn't teach if I didn't, but I can't help thinking that I could do so much more for them, only I don't know how. Sometimes I don't think I'll ever understand what's going on in school . . . what makes kids act the way they do.'

'What makes you say that?' said Colin. 'Has something happened?'

And so she began to tell Colin about the tearful Gary as she sipped her Campari. Over the lasagne she moved on to tell him about the apparently innumerate Sarah and about Eileen the 'superteacher', saving her indignation concerning her visit to the secondary school for the veal cutlets in milanese sauce. Finally, she rounded off her tale of woe by describing the incident in the train involving Sharon and her mum, as she finished her favourite dessert, zabaglione.

As they sipped their coffee and liqueurs, Colin (who was an educational psychologist) asked her if she knew anything about the behavioural approach to teaching. Taking the incidents she had reported as examples, he then went on to show her how they could all be more easily understood within a framework based on behavioural psychology. Moreover, this approach had obvious implications for action. By learning more about behavioural psychology, Colin maintained, and then applying it in the classroom, one could become a much more effective teacher. Jan listened carefully.

'You know', she began, 'if what you say is right, then you ought to write a book about it for teachers like me . . .'

EXERCISE

Before we move on to provide an overview of the behavioural approach to teaching let us take some more examples of classroom teaching problems, this time in the form of a quick quiz. Study the following fairly common situations and decide which one of the alternative approaches suggested most closely resembles what you might do in similar circumstances or what you would advise the teacher to do.

1.   Sally usually works fairly hard, and her work is of quite a good standard, but recently she has taken to spending whole lessons gazing out of the window daydreaming. Her teacher wants to try to break her of this habit. Should he:

(a)   permit the daydreams as long as they do not last too long?
(b)   try to ensure that something interesting happens in the classroom when she is not attending, in order to get her attention?
(c)   tell her he will have to see her parents if she does not stop?
(d)   watch Sally until she appears to be attending and then praise her for that?

(*e*) get another child to watch her to tell him when she is not attending?

2. Jane is very much of a 'loner' and rarely plays or talks with the other children. Her teacher feels that she ought to have more to do with the others. Should the teacher:

(*a*) force Jane to participate with the others by asking the other children to talk to her more?
(*b*) try to find something that Jane can do better than most of the others and get her to help children who are less able than herself?
(*c*) get Jane and the others to talk it over in class?
(*d*) wait until Jane shows even the faintest sign of interest in another child and praise her every time it happens?
(*e*) take the pressure off Jane by leaving her alone?

3. Mark is the 'star' of the class. His work and behaviour are both excellent. One day his teacher hears him complaining to a friend that the teacher never takes any notice of him or praises him. Should the teacher:

(*a*) in future, keep telling Mark how clever he is?
(*b*) explain to Mark that she does appreciate him really, but that she needs to spend more time with those who find learning very hard?
(*c*) make sure that he gets a star for each piece of work handed in?
(*d*) make sure that he gets a star for good work or behaviour every now and then?
(*e*) continue as before, since his work and behaviour are good?

4. Class 4 simply cannot come in and sit down quietly after games. Their teacher is determined to try to improve their behaviour. Should she:

(*a*) try to locate the notable troublemakers and explain why they need to come in quietly?
(*b*) punish those who are noisy or silly?
(*c*) explain to the whole class why they should behave better on every occasion when somebody is silly?
(*d*) concentrate first upon rewarding those children who can at least come in quietly?

(*e*)   tell them that they will not have games until they can learn to behave better?

5.   Every day the teacher has to take the register against a background of noise. When she tells the class off they are quiet, but as soon as she re-starts the register the noise rises again. Should she:

(*a*)   ignore the talking and speed up taking the register?
(*b*)   reorganise the class so that the register is not taken in such a formal situation?
(*c*)   try to spot those who are talking and isolate them?
(*d*)   assign a simple task to be done during registration (for example, read a book) and reward those who comply?
(*e*)   keep the whole class in until the register can be taken in peace and quiet?

6.   Barry often shouts out the answers to questions without being asked. Should his teacher:

(*a*)   threaten to send him to the headmaster when he does this?
(*b*)   take him on one side and explain that it is not polite to shout out?
(*c*)   keep him in at break as a punishment?
(*d*)   ignore shouted answers but praise him when he raises his hand?
(*e*)   always address questions to individual pupils by name?

We hope that this exercise encouraged you to think about general strategies for approaching these problems. There are, of course, no right answers in any absolute sense. One of the points we must emphasise is that there are no foolproof, fixed procedures which will always work in all situations with all children. Although we will provide some 'recipes' which have been demonstrated to produce good results in certain circumstances, like good cooks we must be both creative and able to adapt easily to situations where ingredients and equipment are different. In other words, one needs to know something about the underlying theory, the methodology and the technology of the behavioural approach to teaching in order to be a good teacher, just as we need to know the same things about cooking in order to be a good cook.

In general terms, if you tend to pick alternative *d* most of the time you are probably already practising, or are at least aware of, some of the principles which we will be discussing. But please do not stop reading! We all have something to learn, even headteachers! Even if you always 'instinctively' use alternative *d* type strategies you will probably find it even more useful if you can place your techniques within an appropriate theoretical framework. This is likely to lead to still more effective teaching.

If you picked few alternative *d* strategies, do not despair. Some of the other alternatives might also be helpful in certain circumstances but try to work out how the '*d*' alternatives are similar in the solutions they offer. In this book we aim to teach you both *why* such strategies work and also *how* to go about implementing them. You will have noticed that alternative *d* strategies generally involve rewarding children's behaviour which we want to encourage. In keeping with this point of view, perhaps you could now reward yourself with a cup of tea or coffee for having taken the initiative to improve your teaching and for having read the first chapter!

Chapter 2

An Overview of the Behavioural Approach to Teaching

The behavioural approach to teaching is based on behavioural psychology, which rests upon a number of general assumptions. They may be summarised as follows:

(1) The concern of psychology (and hence of teaching) is with the observable.

This means that teachers who adopt the behavioural approach (behavioural teachers) concern themselves with what a child actually does, that is, his behaviour, rather than speculating about unconscious motives or the processes underlying his behaviour. The behavioural approach is objective and is concerned with the observable facts of life. For example, a teacher might report that 'Sally worked well for the first half of the lesson but then her concentration lapsed'. In behavioural terms what happened was that Sally completed ten sums correctly in the first twenty minutes of the lesson, but only two in the last twenty minutes. The teacher's reference to her concentration lapse is an attempt at explanation based purely on speculation.

(2) For the most part, and certainly for most practical purposes, behaviour is learned.

In other words behaviour, what people do, is assumed to have been learned as a result of the individual interacting with his environment, rather than being inherited at birth. This does not mean that behavioural psychologists and teachers *do not* believe in genetic inheritance or that they *do* believe that anybody can be taught to do anything given time. Rather they believe that genetics or biological endowment may set the limits for what an individual can learn, but that behaviour is still the result of learning. In other words, they take the practical view that there is very little you can do about a child's genetic inheritance or the biological state of his nervous system, but that you can make it easier for him to learn behaviours by exercising control over his environment.

(3)   Learning means change in behaviour.

This follows from the first point really. The only way we know (that we *can* know) that learning has taken place is by observing changes in a child's behaviour. The behavioural teacher will not be satisfied with claims such as 'I think she has a better attitude to school now'; he will only be satisfied if the child now displays behaviour(s) which she was not showing before. For example, this might be reflected in her increased attendance and/or punctuality figures.

(4)   Such changes in behaviour (that is, learning) are governed primarily by the 'law of effect'.

In simple terms this means that children (and adults, and other animals for that matter) learn on the basis of tending to repeat behaviours which are followed by consequences which they find desirable or rewarding; similarly they tend not to repeat behaviours the consequences of which they find aversive or punishing. In other words, the consequences of behaviour are critical to learning.

(5)   Behaviours are also governed by the contexts in which they occur.

In any situation some behaviours are more appropriate than others and we learn which situations are appropriate for which behaviour(s). If a child's behaviour is appropriate for the circumstances in which it occurs it is likely to be rewarded; if it occurs in inappropriate circumstances reward is less likely and the behaviour may even lead to punishing consequences. As a result of this we rapidly learn not only how to perform a certain behaviour, but *when* and *where* to perform it. For example, the new boy in the secondary school will soon learn to cheer on the school team from the touchline but merely to clap politely when the result is announced in assembly.

The five points set out above may be seen as the essential features of the behavioural approach to teaching. In large part they derive from the psychology of B. F. Skinner, whose operant learning theory has been very influential. Operant psychology is a science of behaviour which looks for functional, that is to say, causal relationships between behaviours and factors in the environment. As we have already said, this approach assumes that almost all of the behaviour with which we are likely to be concerned is *learned*, and that it is learned and maintained by environmental consequences. The direct application of this to teaching lies in the fact that if we can change or control environmental consequences especially the reactions of other people, then we can change or control children's behaviour. It is important to emphasise, however, that the situations in which a child finds himself will also influence his behaviour and that we can also change the child's behaviour by altering other aspects of his environment. This point is frequently overlooked but is, in fact, extremely important as we shall see.

TEACHING IS ABOUT CHANGING CHILDREN'S BEHAVIOUR

If we believe that teaching is concerned with helping children to learn new skills and gain new information and, if we believe also that learning implies a change or changes in behaviour, then it follows logically that teaching is about changing children's behaviour(s), whether social or academic. Moreover, if teaching is about changing behaviour then the role of the teacher is, quite simply, to bring about changes in the behaviour of the children in her class.

There are many points which we will need to discuss which follow directly from this premiss but let us initially establish the scope of this book; what we are trying to cover and what we are not attempting to present in the context of this short introductory text. Basically, our concern is with the classroom management of children's social behaviour. The behavioural approach may also be applied in curriculum design and in the teaching of academic skills and subject matter but we will not be directly concerned with these aspects here. We must immediately stress, however, that improved social behaviour in the classroom has enormous implications for children's academic progress. Our aim will be to present a positive approach to the perennial problem of classroom discipline and to demonstrate how the behavioural approach yields benefits for teachers and children. By employing effective, positive behavioural methods of establishing control in the classroom, the teacher is freed in large part from the often time-consuming chore of chiding children for disrupting lessons or for not getting on with their work. The teacher is then able to spend more of her time planning and directing effective lessons and advising and explaining with individual children. As a result of this we might also expect children, once they have become consistently more successful at their lessons, to begin to find their schoolwork rewarding in its own right. This is a change in behaviour of a different order and is the ultimate aim of all good teaching. Before we discuss this further, however, it is important to consider briefly some of the basic principles underlying the behavioural approach. Remember that in this chapter we are providing an overview and that many of these points will be covered in more detail later in the book.

THE BEHAVIOURAL TEACHER'S ABC

The behavioural approach to teaching is based on several principles, some of which we have already referred to briefly. The basic model embodying the crucial elements of the behavioural approach is known as the three-term analysis of behaviour or the ABC model.

A refers to the *antecedent* conditions, that is, the context in which a behaviour occurs or what is happening in that environment prior to a behaviour occurring.

B refers to the *behaviour* itself, that is, what a child is actually doing in real physical terms (not what you think might be going on as a result of inferences from his behaviour).

C refers to the *consequences* of the behaviour, that is, what happens to the child after he behaves in a certain way.

ABC is a convenient way of remembering the constituents of the three-term analysis of behaviour and the logical sequence of antecedent, behaviour and consequence. For reasons other than sheer perversity, however, we will not consider them in this order here, but will start with B, the behaviour, since behaviour is the primary concern of the whole approach.

Behaviour

What do we mean when we talk about a child's behaviour? And why do we place such great emphasis on specifying exactly what behaviour a child is displaying? These questions are fundamental to the behavioural approach. Behaviourism as a philosophy of science arose as a reaction to the highly speculative approach of early psychologists who attempted to 'explain' man's behaviour by recourse to inborn 'instincts' and to irrational, uncontrollable, unconscious forces within man. J. B. Watson, the founding father of behaviourism, rejected such notions as vague and untestable and demanded that the study of man should be based on the observable. Consequently he advocated that behaviour should be studied directly, since it can be observed objectively.

We have already said that a child's behaviour refers to what she is actually *doing* and we attempt to say what a child is doing in as precise a way as possible. If we observe a child building a tower with bricks, we would not write down 'creative play' since another observer or someone else reading our notes might interpret 'creative play' differently. It is too vague and imprecise. We would record that the child constructed a tower of four bricks. To say that it is 'creative' and/or that it is 'play' is to interpret, is prone to inaccuracy and vagueness and is unlikely to be useful. Similarly, if a teacher tells us that Jason is always 'messing about' in class, we have to ask the teacher to define the behaviour more clearly. What one teacher regards as 'messing about' may be a far cry from the view of another. Moreover, if we use a vague definition there is no guarantee that it is the same sort of behaviour we are categorising in this way two days running. So we would ask the teacher to list any of Jason's behaviours which he finds objectionable and then to define them as precisely as possible. A behaviour which is frequently found at the top of many teachers' lists is 'talking out of turn'. If we define this as 'any talking by a child when the teacher has requested the class to get on with set work in silence', then we are moving closer towards an objective definition. The more objective our definition the easier it is for two observers to agree that a certain behaviour has occurred and the easier it is to count instances of such behaviour. Counting instances of behaviour can be an extremely useful, if not essential, component of the behavioural approach to teaching, as we shall see later in this book.

Precise definition of behaviour also helps us to avoid the danger of over-interpretation and giving non-explanations as causes of behaviour. Non-explanations sometimes take the form of what are known as *explanatory fictions*. These are generally unhelpful whilst providing a veneer or gloss of 'scientific' explanation. They can also be dangerous in so far as they can be used to label a child.

Labelling is often coupled with the assumption that little can be done about it; the problem is seen as the child and not his behaviour. For example, if Darren keeps hitting other children his teacher may describe him as being aggressive, but if we ask her how she knows this, she may reply, 'He keeps hitting other children'. The word 'aggressive' is simply a label for a child who frequently hits other children but is sometimes used as if it were an explanation of this behaviour. Further examples of explanatory fictions will be presented later.

Consequences

The next item in the three-term analysis is C, for consequences. As we said earlier, this refers to the fact that we tend to repeat behaviours which bring us what we want and to refrain from repeating behaviours leading to occurrences which we want to avoid. This appears to be a characteristic of all animals but we differ from animals, and also from each other, in terms of what we seek out and what we seek to avoid. In common with other animals, we tend to seek out food and will repeat behaviours which have led to the provision of food when we are deprived of it. Moreover, many, if not most of us, will work for money. Similarly, the majority of people find praise and approval rewarding and tend to behave in a way which is likely to be followed by praise or approval. On the other hand, perhaps few of us go out of our way to collect train numbers and, thankfully and more seriously, even fewer seek out and behave in a way likely to secure the 'reward' of drugs such as heroin. A major concern within the behavioural approach to teaching is with the identification of things and events which children find rewarding and to structure the teaching environment so as to make access to these rewards dependent upon behaviour which the teacher wants to encourage in his class. Since this is obviously a major issue we will return to it in more detail later. At this stage, however, it is important to attempt to provide a summary of the effects of the various types of consequence upon behaviour.

In simple, everyday language consequences may be described as 'rewarding' or 'punishing'. Rewarding consequences, which we call *positive reinforcers*, are events which we seek out or 'go for', whilst we try to avoid punishing consequences; neutral consequences are events which affect us neither way. Behaviours followed by positive reinforcers are likely to increase in frequency. Behaviours followed by *punishment* tend to decrease in frequency whilst neutral consequences have no effect. In the behavioural approach to teaching, infrequent but desired behaviours (for example, getting on with the set work quietly) are made more frequent by arranging for positive reinforcers, such as teacher attention and approval, to follow their occurrence. Undesired behaviours may be decreased in frequency by ensuring that positive reinforcers do *not* follow their occurrence, that is, a neutral consequence is arranged. Occasionally it may be necessary to follow undesired

	TO INCREASE BEHAVIOUR(S)	TO DECREASE BEHAVIOUR(S)
DELIVERY OF	'Good things', i.e. rewarding with smiles, sweets, toys, praise, etc. Technical term: Positive reinforcement	'Bad things', i.e. punishing with smacks, frowns, reprimands, etc. Technical term: Punishment
REMOVAL OF	'Bad things', i.e. allowing escape from pain, noise, nagging, threats, etc. Technical term: Negative reinforcement	'Good things', i.e. losing privileges, house points, money, opportunities to earn 'good things', etc. Technical term: Response cost

Figure 2.1   *The relationships between consequences and their effects.*

behaviours with punishers (for example, a stern 'telling off') in an attempt to reduce the frequency of behaviour rapidly, but there are many problems associated with this procedure. Contrary to popular belief, punishment plays only a minor and infrequent role in the behavioural approach, not least because what we believe to be punishing could, in fact, be reinforcing to the child. For example, the child who receives little attention from adults may behave in ways which result in adult disapproval. This child may prefer disapproval to being ignored and will continue to behave like this because adult attention is positively reinforcing. This is known as *attention-seeking behaviour*.

We should note that terminating a punishing consequence is also reinforcing and can be, and often is, used to increase desired behaviours. This is known as *negative reinforcement*. Again this has problems associated with its use since the child may rapidly learn other, more effective, ways of avoiding the negative consequence than the one you had in mind. For example, a teacher may continually use sarcasm and ridicule with his pupils. He ceases only when they behave as he wishes. Another way of avoiding this unpleasant consequence, however, other than by doing as the teacher wishes, is to stay away from school. Finally, one can punish by removing or terminating positive consequences (for example, by taking away a child's sweets). This is known as *response cost* but again there are similar problems associated with this approach. Figure 2.1 shows the relationships between these various consequences and their effects.

It is important to remember that at this stage we are attempting only to provide an overview of the general behavioural approach. We will have much more to say about consequences and the technical definitions of what constitutes a punisher or a reinforcer later in this book. We must now, however, turn to the remaining aspect of the ABC model, A or the antecedent conditions.

Antecedents

It is not sufficient to attempt to examine behaviour simply in terms of behaviours and reinforcers. As well as considering what happens after a behaviour occurs (the consequence) we must also consider what happened before the behaviour occurred. We must examine events which precede as well as events which follow behaviour. Events which precede behaviour and/or the settings in which it occurs are known as antecedent stimuli or conditions.

Some school situations provide good examples of such settings. Cookery rooms provide special settings in which the number of children permitted is small, where there is a lot of special apparatus of a practical nature and where the expected activities allow more physical freedom than in most other classrooms. If a teacher of French, say, is obliged to use such a practical room he will encounter special difficulties not only from the unsuitability and insufficiency of the furniture and its layout but also because of the way children are accustomed to respond in this special setting. Being in the cookery room has become associated with a different form of behaviour involving more movement about the room. Sometimes the settings themselves constrain and limit responses. If the temperature is too low one cannot concentrate on the task; if the lighting is too dim or too bright one cannot see. If the classroom is experienced as a cold place there will tend to be a scramble for places near to the radiator. Similarly, crowding may influence children's behaviour. For example, it has been shown that nursery children pay more attention to a story when they have plenty of space than when they are allowed to crowd around their teacher.

We can take another example which highlights how antecedent events influence behaviour. The teacher asks a child a question in class (the antecedent stimulus), the child gives a silly answer (the behaviour) and his classmates laugh (the consequence). If this consequence is positively reinforcing, we may expect the child to produce silly answers upon subsequent similar occasions. He will probably be less likely to do so, however, when his classmates are not there. In other words, the presence of his peers has become a stimulus for his behaviour.

It may be seen from the above examples that antecedents may influence behaviour in two ways. First, there are those antecedent conditions which provide physical constraints or opportunities for behaviours. At its simplest, the physical presence of a football allows ball-kicking (behaviour) to take place. Similarly, overcrowding invites pushing and jostling. Secondly, there are antecedent conditions which have acquired power over behaviour by association with rewarding or punishing consequences. Being in Softy Simpson's room may rapidly become the stimulus for unruly behaviour, for example, whilst few would dare even to breathe loudly in Biffer Barnes's classroom. From the practical point of view, however, these distinctions need not concern us greatly.

All this gives some idea of the need to consider the context in which behaviours occur. The relationships between A, the ante-cedent conditions, B, the behaviours and C, the consequences, are known as the *contingencies of reinforcement*. Another important consideration which we must bear in mind, however, is the *frequency* of reinforcement.

FREQUENCY OF REINFORCEMENT

When we want to teach a child something new, or to encourage him to behave in a certain way more frequently than he normally does, it is important that we ensure that he is positively reinforced *every* time he behaves as we want him to. This normally leads to rapid learning and is known as *continuous reinforcement*. When he has learned the new behaviour and/or is behaving as we want him to do, regularly, then we may maintain this behaviour more economically by reducing the frequency of reinforcement. Another important reason for wanting to reduce the frequency is that the child may become less responsive if the positive reinforcer becomes too easily available. Consequently, once a child is regularly behaving in a desired way we can best maintain that behaviour by ensuring that he is now reinforced only inter-mittently. *Intermittent reinforcement* can be arranged so that a child is reinforced every so often (that is, in terms of time) or, alternatively, after so many occurrences of the behaviour. These different ways of organising the frequency of reinforcement are known as *reinforcement schedules* and will be referred to again.

Following this brief summary of basic behavioural theory, we can now turn to a consideration of what the behavioural approach to teaching is all about. With some children the behaviour that concerns us has not yet been learned, with others the behaviour is learned but does not occur frequently enough whilst other children frequently behave in inappropriate ways. The behavioural approach to teaching is about changing the frequencies of behaviour(s). It can be used to teach new skills or to increase or decrease existing rates of behaviour. It is important to emphasise, however, that the behavioural approach to teaching is primarily concerned with increasing the frequency of desirable behaviour in the classroom.

THE BEHAVIOURAL EXPLANATION OF JAN'S DILEMMA

Now that we have considered the behavioural approach we can take another look at the problems facing Jan, the teacher we met in Chapter 1. It would be a good idea at this point to glance back at the five scenes presented there. Can we now begin to understand what is going on using our knowledge of the behavioural approach so far?

In the first scene she was struggling to make sense of Gary's apparently unpredictable behaviour. Careful observation of exactly what happened would have revealed that the variations in his behaviour were related to the different situations in which he found himself. In other words, our knowledge of the ABC model enables us to see that a changed situation brings about a change in response. Gary has learned that crying in the presence of a sympathetic teacher like Eileen leads to consequences which he finds reinforcing in the form of attention and comforting. On the other hand, the older boys with whom he likes to play, effectively punish, or at least ignore, him when he cries unnecessarily. As a result of this Gary has learned a new, more stoical response to minor injuries when playing with them since they reinforce such behaviour with approval and acceptance. This is a good illustration of the importance of antecedents for behaviour and of how they gain their power through differential consequences.

In scene 1 we also have examples of explanatory fictions and the problems associated with labelling. Jan's friend, Hilary, by referring to Gary as a 'great strapping lad', shows that she has certain expectations of the way in which he will behave. By labelling in this way we signal our expectations and then tend to focus mainly on aspects of behaviour which confirm them. When Hilary's labelling of Gary comes unstuck she resorts to an explanatory fiction. Gary is labelled 'mardy'. (How does she know he is 'mardy'? Because he cries so easily. Why does he cry so easily? Because he is 'mardy'.) We can see easily enough that explanatory fictions like this merely provide a circular argument and are non-explanations of behaviour.

In scene 2 we may note some more very good examples of explanatory fictions. Hilary demonstrates clearly how teachers use such explanations and how stubbornly they will stick to them in order to justify themselves. She refers to a block about maths and to number-blindness. Even when Jan, trying to be a little more objective, considers Sarah's output rather than her attitude and supposed application, Hilary is not to be moved, saying, 'Well, maybe she's just a bit slow then, a bit backward perhaps'.

Jan's 'bad lads' provide us with another good model for observing the power of antecedents. These lads who were so troublesome the year before are now, apparently, prepared to work hard and so cause little bother. However, this has not been brought about by the application of some magic formula. Some antecedents gain their power, as we suggested, from association with certain consequences. We can see the sort of consequences Eileen provides when we 'overhear' her comments, 'Well done, class 3. That's what I like to see', and so on. Jan falls into the trap of supposing that Eileen's ability to use positive reinforcement so effectively is an inborn gift; that some people are born teachers, in fact. There is no doubt that although Jan and Eileen may have been somewhat different temperamentally at birth, Eileen had to *learn* to use praise and attention as positive reinforcers. She also had to *learn* to apply these contingently so as to derive the maximum effect in the classroom and doubtless this is a skill she has acquired since becoming a teacher. Whilst Jan appears to be focusing her attention on bad behaviour, Eileen concentrates her social reinforcement on good outcomes on the part of Jan's previously 'bad lads'. (We should note, however, that even 'natural' behavioural teachers like Eileen still have room for improvement; remember, it was Eileen who was unwittingly reinforcing Gary's 'mardy' behaviour.) It is more than likely that if Jan were, for some reason, to take her old class back from Eileen and into her old room to teach them, the famous 'bad lads' would soon begin to live up to their former reputations and to reproduce much of their old troublesome behaviour; such is the power of antecedent stimuli. In this scene, too, we have Jan referring to these boys first as 'bad lads' and then as having 'grown up', when all the while they are responding quite naturally to the contingencies of reinforcement as explained by the ABC model. Here, again, we can see how teachers, and others, tend to use labelling as a way of explaining and justifying what they observe.

In scene 3 we focus on the nature of punishment. This secondary school teacher is using what he believes to be aversive consequences to control his pupils. He accuses Adams of not knowing what punishment is, yet clearly his use of it displays his own ignorance. His use of sarcasm, mixed with schoolboy witticisms, is not only ineffective as a punisher but, in a sense, provides a stimulus for disruption. He is placing his pupils in a 'double bind' situation by providing a stimulus, inviting them to laugh at his 'wit' and, at the same time, daring them to challenge his authority. Much of Adams's behaviour is being controlled not by the teacher at all but by the attention of his peers; a very powerful reinforcer in the classroom. This is illustrated well when the teacher uses sexually loaded phrases like 'kick against the pricks', which brings a reaction from the class. The teacher reacts in turn to their disruptive laughter which reinforces this still further. His complete failure to understand the nature of punishment is demonstrated in the last paragraph but one in this scene where he attempts to define what is funny or otherwise. He goes on by referring to the fact that Adams is in detention for the third time in one week and then equates this with punishment. Behaviourally, we might have to consider detention, as defined for Adams, as something other than punishment since it is clearly not reducing the behaviour for which it is being awarded.

This teacher also attempts to use sarcasm as a negative reinforcer. It normally works by the teacher withdrawing the sarcasm as soon as the class or the individual ceases behaving badly. In this case, however, the teacher, through his inconsistent behaviour, allows and even encourages the class to laugh, thus nullifying its effect. In a sort of cat and mouse game, created by the teacher, he and the class are maintaining each others' behaviour(s). It should be noted that for the duration of the incident the class do no academic work at all.

Scene 4 describes learning in the family situation. The interest of the children in, to them, new objects in the environment is not shared by their parents. Parental attention to these interesting objects can be brought about only by successively louder and more persistent demands. This teaches the children, by degrees, to increase the level of their behaviour until the parent has to respond. The response, when it comes, is what to most people would appear to be aversive. However, since it is not choking off the behaviour (Jan watched the fifth action replay in her short journey), it must be positively reinforcing. In other words, attention, even of an aversive nature, from the parents of young children is preferred to no attention at all. It should be noted that these children have been taught by their parents to be very persistent in their demanding behaviour. They have learned that *eventually* the parents will give in. These children have thus been taught by their parents to engage and persist in behaviour which would be highly aversive to most adults, simply to gain their attention. It is interesting to note that the father's lack of attention to his daughter's importuning extends also to his wife who has to use the same escalation techniques to get his ear. Behaviour such as this will tend to generalise to the school situation, where it will be entirely unsuitable, quite different social skills being called for. Children such as these will soon acquire reputations for inability to sit still or talk quietly and for bad behaviour generally. If such labels are applied they will tend to be self-fulfilling for both children and teachers.

In the last scene we can observe how people who are close to each other mutually reinforce aspects of behaviour which appeal to them and give reinforcement in return: a mutually reinforcing relationship using naturally occurring events. For example, Colin uses an obvious compliment to get Jan started and would then provide many facial expressions, gestures and body movements of a very subtle nature to encourage her to go on to recount her troubles. He uses verbal prompts, too. After a suitable interval he then proceeds to put the day's events into a behavioural context as we have been doing in the last few paragraphs in order to provide a better framework for her understanding of the problems of the classroom teacher.

POSSIBLE CRITICISMS AND OBJECTIONS

Before moving on it is important, at this stage, to consider some of the possible criticisms or objections to the behavioural approach. First, assuming that we can do so, what right does any of us have to interfere with the behaviour of another person? If the behavioural view is correct and our behaviour is modified by its consequences then that process goes on all the time whether we are aware of it or not and whether it is done consciously or not. So by removing a particular conscious effort to control the behaviour of another person we do not leave that person free to behave as he wishes; we leave him subject to naturally occurring consequences which may or may not teach him adaptive social behaviours. Children who are not taught how to ask for things politely through guiding and praising will still learn to get what they want, but by snatching and grabbing. Similarly, we can systematically teach children how to gain our attention in an acceptable way but if we do not, they will learn other, almost certainly less desirable ways. Whatever children learn has been taught mainly by the consequences we provide, whether consciously or not.

Children are not born with ready-made behavioural repertoires. They have to learn them, and it is mainly their parents who help them in this through providing them with realistic guidelines for their behaviours in social situations. Most children come to school with well-developed and adaptive repertoires of behaviour which enable them to settle easily into the school and to continue the educative process with success. Some, however, do not and the teacher will have to do her best to eliminate some of their inappropriate behaviours altogether. Some behaviours she will have to encourage because although present they do not occur at a high enough rate, whilst other behaviours she will have to teach from scratch. This calls for thoughtful intervention from the teacher and its justification lies entirely in the judgement of what is in the child's best interests. The teacher, acting in loco parentis, is paid to bring about changes in the child's behaviour which will allow him to get the best out of life. What the child needs is to learn a wide repertoire of skills so that whatever situation he finds himself in he will have a wide choice of options for behaving. This is the teachers' justification for *teaching* whatever the means used, behavioural or otherwise.

Another criticism applies to all novel forms of remediation. If we believe that we have a remedy for a person's problem and are in the position to administer it, then the question becomes, 'What right have we to with-hold it?' This is a situation often faced in medicine when a remedy has been found but is, as yet, not properly tested out. Many sufferers want to try it on the off-chance that it may work for them and without side-effects.

The advocate of a particular form of treatment may feel justified in employing it but his task is to convince others that he is so justified. One of the great strengths of the behavioural approach is its complete openness. It makes totally manifest, throughout, exactly what is being looked at, counted, recorded and charted. It states exactly what behaviour is to be changed, setting out the criteria to be met at each stage. It describes just what strategy is being used and what effect it is having and defines with clarity the end product – the behaviour which it is seeking to bring about. By comparison many other approaches surround themselves with a mystique. They attempt to elevate their practitioners suggesting that the layman cannot understand the inner mysteries of their 'science'. They disclose neither their diagnosis nor their remedies and allow themselves alone to pass judgement on the 'cure'.

Those who espouse the 'medical model' are frequently of this type. Advocates of the medical model frequently criticise those who adopt a behavioural approach on the grounds that they are merely attempting to treat the symptoms (the behaviour) rather than the underlying problem itself. Such approaches, they claim, are akin to prescribing aspirin for toothache, which alleviates the symptoms (pain) but leaves the real cause (a rotten tooth) untreated. As a result of this, they would argue, other symptoms (problems) will inevitably surface sooner or later (for example, swelling due to an abscess). In classroom terms this would be illustrated by a child who, when taught to remain seated instead of wandering about the classroom, will now begin calling out to the teacher or displaying other unwanted behaviours, since the cause is left untreated. This is known as *symptom substitution*. So-called 'causes' might include, for example, hyperactivity, minimal brain damage, or early weaning.

In response to this, advocates of the behavioural approach would make several points:

(*a*) that the behaviour *is* the problem;
(*b*) that 'deeper' causes are frequently difficult to identify and often take the form of explanatory fictions; and
(*c*) that there is no evidence for symptom substitution.

In sum, the behavioural approach concerns itself with the observable. There are no inner mysteries, the approach is direct and the outcomes clear. In the final analysis we point to our success rate in achieving enduring changes in behaviour without any evidence for symptom substitution or any other side-effects.

Another issue on which we must comment is that of bribery. Because extrinsic rewards are used widely in the behavioural approach the method is sometimes accused of employing bribery. However, this position cannot be upheld since bribes are usually given before the required behaviour whereas positive reinforcement is always consequential, that is, it is given after and only if the appropriate behaviour has occurred. In addition, bribes are usually given for some illegal or undesirable behaviour where a person has to be persuaded to overcome his scruples. On the other hand, positive reinforcement, within the behavioural approach to teaching, is always employed to bring about outcomes which are for the subject's eventual benefit. In the same way that the behavioural approach draws a distinction between a 'bad boy' (which could become self-fulfilling) and bad behaviour, so it draws another between 'I will give you . . . provided that . . .', which constitutes bribery, and 'When you do this, then . . .', which is a contractual reinforcement. Would a reasonable person regard the action of removing one's hand from a red hot surface as a response to bribery? Alternatively, how many of us regard our weekly or monthly pay packet as a bribe and would be prepared to go on working without its prospect?

Another problematical issue concerns the situation in which the teacher is treating one child only within a group. Some teachers fear that this will bring about a certain jealousy among the rest or that they will begin to say to themselves, 'Arthur is getting rewards because he is behaving better but we behave like that all the time. Let's start behaving badly so that we can be rewarded for improvement.' This is a highly sophisticated response but it really misses the main point. Children who are behaving in ways that are socially acceptable are doing so because their actions are being maintained by the reinforcement contingencies which are operating for them. If the teacher feels that one child needs special help then others in the group may have to be involved. Children, despite their insistence upon fairness, do not equate this with equality in treatment. They are realists and can make a real contribution to a programme which will help another child, especially where peer group reaction is maintaining a behaviour. If this is believed to be impossible then there are two alternatives. The programme applied to the individual, or at least the rewarding sequence, must be made surreptitious; alternatively, the rest of the group must be allowed to benefit from the individual's success. If the subject's success results in every member of the group sharing in the reward, then peer influence is likely to be supportive towards the programme. Where social acceptance of the subject by the group is the aim, the actual handing over of rewards by the subject can be used as part of the programme. If the whole class is getting some reward consequent on the behaviour of one of its members, then *that* child can be the one to give out the reward.

The teacher's judgement is called into play whenever ethical issues are raised. If it can be agreed that teaching is concerned with bringing about changes in children's behaviour, then it is only a matter of deciding which behaviours need changing. This is a task which the teacher has to fulfil in any case as part of her daily duty. She has to decide which method should be used. Here, the main criterion would seem to be effectiveness in terms of effort expended, a matter of pure economy. An open-minded person cannot but agree that the behavioural approach offers an attractive alternative for the busy teacher.

EXERCISES

Before we begin to spell out in greater detail the implication of all this for classroom management we provide two quite straightforward exercises by means of which you can test your own understanding of some of the basic ideas that we have dealt with so far.

1.   Which of these statements is consistent with the behavioural approach?

(*a*)   Some people are born able to concentrate and some are not.
(*b*)   Teachers change children's behaviour and since they are paid to do so they should do it well.
(*c*)   If children behave badly then it is because they have failed to learn.
(*d*)   Children should be allowed to develop naturally and choose their own ways of behaving.
(*e*)   Positive techniques are more effective in teaching than methods which include punishment.
(*f*)   Children with low IQs cannot be taught anything worthwhile.
(*g*)   Teachers have no right to change children's attitudes and values.
(*h*)   It is quite natural for children to behave differently at home from the way they do at school.

2.   Some of the statements below are behavioural explanations whilst some are 'explanatory fictions'. Can you work out which are which?

(*a*)   Elsie is more interested in sex than most girls of her age because she has an overactive sex drive.
(*b*)   Johnny plays around in class because the other children laugh at him.
(*c*)   Henry works so slowly because he has a slow working brain.
(*d*)   Joan continually asks her teacher to look at her book since she finds such attention rewarding.
(*e*)   Billy continually wanders around the classroom despite being told off because being told off is not a punishing event for him.
(*f*)   Sally does not seem to be able to learn to read because she is dyslexic.

(*g*)   Mary never volunteers an answer because she is too shy.

(*h*)   Cyril always opens the door for his teacher because he is so well-mannered.

(*i*)   Richard gets on with his work so that his teacher will not shout at him.

The answers, or rather, suggested solutions, to these two exercises are to be found at the back of the book.

Chapter 3

Pinpointing and Recording Children's Behaviour

In the previous chapter we referred to the need for observing and recording children's behaviour in an objective and systematic way. Human behaviour is notoriously difficult to observe because it happens in complex social situations which are also dynamic, that is to say, things are happening all the time. Classrooms are prime examples of such social situations. The purpose of this chapter is to enable you to identify key behaviours in certain children or groups of children by *pinpointing* them so that you will be able to judge precisely when they are happening and can record them accurately and objectively when necessary. In this chapter, then, we shall be looking at B, the behaviour, in the ABC model.

Teachers are concerned with bringing about changes in the behaviour of their pupils because, as we have said, this is what learning implies. At one stage the ability of a child to respond in a certain situation is lacking and then, at a later stage, the response is seen to occur. For instance, at 5-and-a-half the presentation of a page of print leads to no response from a child, but at 6-and-a-half she can read and understand the words of a nursery rhyme. Alternatively, at 7 years a boy swings his bat at a ball which is bowled to him but seldom makes contact. Eighteen months later he can hit any reasonably pitched ball up to 50 yards. Social skills also have to be learned, so that by the age of 5 most children respond with 'Thank you' if they are given something to eat, but they were certainly not born with that skill.

All such skill-learning, whether social, physical, or academic, has to be judged according to the context in which it occurs. Children sometimes use their skills for inappropriate purposes, for example, writing graffiti on walls, throwing or hitting stones or balls through windows, and so on. Within the context of the classroom, teachers are able to judge the appropriateness of skills with some accuracy. In fact, they are paid for making such judgements and for guiding their pupils along fairly well-defined pathways. Generally, they see their task as one of teaching appropriate academic skills and making certain academic knowledge available. For this to happen most children require a specific social context: a context of order and reasonable quietness which it is the teacher's job to initiate and maintain.

Before a teacher can decide whether she needs to take action over a certain behaviour she must decide upon the appropriateness of it in the classroom context. The behaviour of most children in the classroom may well be fairly satisfactory but every teacher will meet some pupils who have academic or behavioural problems. Before she begins to intervene, the teacher must be able to justify her actions in terms of the long-term effects for her pupils. Some pupil behaviour may be annoying to the teacher but not, in itself, harmful. For example, chewing in class, though it may be judged to be disrespectful by some teachers, could not be said to be wrong, unless dietary or other considerations are taken into account. If we can agree that the teacher's main task is to arrange for learning to take place, then within the context of the classroom any behaviour can be judged maladaptive or inappropriate if it:

(1) interferes with the child's own learning;
(2) interferes with the learning of other members of the group; or
(3) prevents the teacher from carrying out her tasks of instructing, explaining, reading, organising, coaching, and so on.

Thus day-dreaming, playing with toys or apparatus, or wandering around the room would certainly interfere with the child's own learning. Talking to others in the group or attacking them or their property would clearly interfere with the learning of others, whilst persistent conduct of this nature would probably demand a great deal of the teacher's time and attention and prevent her from performing her major teaching function. Much of the teacher's concern is to see that the children concentrate or get on with the job in hand: what is known as *on-task* behaviour. If the children are not on-task then the likelihood is that not much learning is going on. In fact, recent research has shown a clear relationship between on-task behaviour and the amount of classwork completed. If we can increase on-task behaviour then at least learning is possible, provided always that the material is appropriate to the child's current skill level. As we have said, the primary concern of this book is with the control of children's social behaviour, which inevitably yields improved academic behaviour.

The behaviour of some children seems to teachers to be almost totally maladaptive. They seldom seem to behave appropriately, whilst their academic output is minimal and of very poor quality. Such children seem to have problems in all academic subjects, whilst their social behaviour puts them in conflict with the standards of most teachers. To many teachers such children appear to be hopeless cases and they just do not know where to start with them. They may begin to look for reasons for this state of affairs and will often end by regarding the parents or the locality as the scape-goats. Teachers sometimes begin to rationalise by commenting that the child's IQ is too low, that the home environment is deprived, that parents have given the child only limited access to language in that they have not talked to him or read to him, and so on. This presents a very gloomy outlook for the child and for the teacher's efforts on his behalf and it ignores some very important principles. These are part of the alternative, behavioural approach which is much more optimistic both for the child and for the teacher.

To begin with, the behavioural approach does not concern itself with inner causes of behaviour such as native ability, expressed as IQ, or a child's will to learn, or his persistence, or any other supposed qualities of character. We referred earlier to such non-explanations as 'explanatory fictions'. For example, the only evidence for a person's persistence is observation of his persistent behaviour in a number of situations. He might then be described as persistent in these situations but persistence is not something that can be *generally* attributed to a person. The teacher may well groan about Charlie's lack of persistence when it comes to a reading task that she has set, but if she could observe some of his other behaviour she would find him acting in remarkably persistent ways. He is always asking his mother for sweets and money. He never gives up until he gets what he wants. The same is true of his bullying behaviour towards other children in the playground and this is despite all sorts of sanctions applied by teachers, dinner supervisors and others. In behavioural terms we would say that Charlie has learned these behaviours in particular contexts through the consequences which have followed them over the preceding months and years. Worrying his mother for sweets always works, eventually; toiling at books has never produced anything at all that gives him pleasure. Being a nuisance in the playground at least makes him a somebody and gets him attention, even if some of the consequences are not too pleasant. Charlie behaves the way he does as a result of the consequences provided by his environment, especially the reactions of other people. The optimistic spin-off to all this is that what the environment has taught can be untaught and that other learning can take its place, this time by conscious planning.

When we talk about other children we use phrases like 'well-mannered', 'studious', or 'considerate'. The behavioural teacher, without denying that there are differences in temperament and rates of learning which may be seen from the earliest stages of development, would explain these differences in terms of learning. No child was born well-mannered; in any case what is well-mannered in one society could well turn out to be thoroughly unacceptable in another. Children learn to be well-mannered because in the society in which they happen to be brought up, such responses bring rewarding consequences from the people around them. In the same way, the child who is able to concentrate on his books does so because in the past such behaviour has brought reinforcing consequences for him. What these consequences are likely to be is not always predictable.

Another optimistic aspect of the behavioural approach is that we look directly at the behaviour and not at the person who is behaving. The child exhibiting maladaptive behaviour is simply behaving 'naturally' in response to certain environmental conditions. The behaviour may very well be 'bad' in our terms but the child is not. To tell him that he is bad may cause us to fall into the 'labelling trap'. In other words, we shall subsequently expect him to behave badly and will tend to pay attention to such behaviour thereby reinforcing it, whereas we should be attending to his good responses and applying positive consequences in order to increase them. The behavioural approach always concentrates on the *positive* side of things. Its theme is 'accentuate the positive'.

PINPOINTING

To adopt the behavioural approach we have to be able to identify specific behaviours. We have to learn to pick out particular behaviours which we can clearly identify, observe and, if necessary, count. This is what we mean by pinpointing. Suppose we are concerned about a child who day-dreams and thus does not get much work done. In pinpointing we will need to concentrate upon defining exactly what we mean by 'day-dreaming', such as 'gazing away from his exercise-book', but this will not do if he is looking at the blackboard in order to copy the next sentence. Our definition must be watertight so that we can easily recognise the behaviour every time it happens, without requiring too much thought for us to decide whether it is day-dreaming or not. It must certainly avoid vagueness and the inclusion of such terms as 'looks vacant'. We will have to be quite straightforward and say that day-dreaming will include looking anywhere other than at his book or paper, the blackboard (if appropriate) and the teacher, if she is talking to him or the class.

To take another example, perhaps our problem is with the child who always keeps us waiting. The teacher says, 'Stop working' or 'Line up' or 'Get out such and such a book', but *whatever* it is, Ruth is always last, thereby causing endless frustration. In order to pinpoint this behaviour for observing and counting we will have to place an arbitrary time limit on her responding of, say, ten seconds. If she responds to the request within that time, well and good. If not, then we score one pinpointed event. Here we have set up a clear criterion for scoring which can be readily understood.

In the two examples given above we have concentrated on pinpointing troublesome behaviours so that we can gain an accurate impression of their frequency by counting carefully defined examples of their occurrence. It is even more important to be able to pinpoint precisely the behaviours we want to encourage since it is this positive outlook, focusing as it does on reinforcing examples of good behaviour, which characterises the behavioural approach to teaching. So, if we decide that we would like all of the children in our class to contribute to a discussion session in an acceptable way, we might pinpoint the desired behaviour as 'raising the hand and waiting to be asked to speak'. Another useful behaviour to pinpoint is 'getting on with your work'. We often refer to this behaviour as being 'on task'. Conversely, 'off-task' refers to the child doing something incompatible with getting on with his work. We would attempt to pinpoint on-task behaviour in terms of the task in hand. If, for example, the children are completing work-cards this could include: looking at (reading) the work-card, writing in their exercise-books, looking at the teacher when she is giving instructions, colouring or tracing, and so on, as demanded by the work-card. 'Off-task' would include behaviours usually regarded as incompatible with such work. These might include being out of seat (without permission), chattering (unless the set task involves discussion), gazing into space, disturbing other children, doodling, and so on.

You will have noticed that the units pinpointed are, in themselves, very small: small particular actions or responses, not complex sequences of events which might be difficult to identify. Counting these small units enables us to identify small changes in behaviour, which are what we shall be interested in, especially at first. Another basic principle of the approach is to tackle one behaviour at a time. Some children, as mentioned above, seem to have so many problems that teachers do not know where to start, but we have to be patient and attempt to improve just one behaviour initially. Experience has shown that this is the most effective way, even though it may not appear to be so at first sight. Frequently, a single problem, tackled systematically, is found to have spin-off effects on other troublesome behaviours. When a programme begins to work, the child, maybe for the first time that he can remember, is reinforced for behaviour of which his teacher approves and this can have a remarkable effect.

Whilst we are pinpointing behaviours which we feel are needing our intervention, it is also important to consider what we are aiming at: in other words, what our ultimate goal is. We might want to increase the neatness of this child's work output or decrease the other's talking, but we would not expect the former to work for 100 per cent of the time nor a total cessation of talking in the other. We all have 'off days' and we all talk out of turn on occasion. It is important to keep in mind the definition of maladaptiveness with which we started. Our aim is to produce children who display acceptable levels of behaviour which will be maintained by the normal reinforcement contingencies operating in classrooms and schools. We are not in the business of trying to produce saints who never misbehave or robots who are programmed to do only what they have been told. Not only would this be unnatural; it would be impossible.

RECORD-KEEPING

Once you have pinpointed a behaviour to your satisfaction you will need to devise a simple way to count and record it when it occurs. It is important to keep such a record for three main reasons. First, this information will help you to decide whether you need to take any action. It is often the case, when a teacher has recorded instances of some 'problem behaviour', that the records show the frequency of the behaviour to be far less than had been supposed. In other words, the teacher's judgement has been at fault and, in fact, no intervention is necessary. Sometimes, the fact that a teacher begins to count and record a behaviour has an effect of its own. The child's habitual, annoying behaviour just ceases, as if by magic. It could be that the teacher's response to the behaviour, by virtue of observing and counting its occurrence, has changed and has, in turn, brought about a change in the target behaviour. This phenomenon is sometimes called the 'disappearing problem'.

Secondly, if you decide that an intervention is necessary to bring about a change in behaviour then your continued record-keeping will allow you to judge whether you are being effective. Daily record-keeping, for example, in which children are observed for short periods, provides immediate and constant feedback on the effects of your intervention. If it is not working you will know at once and can modify it. If it *is* working, again you will know and can begin to make changes so that the improved behaviour will be maintained.

Thirdly, careful record-keeping will enable you to identify the settings within which these behaviours occur most frequently. For instance, Frank, who keeps getting out of his seat, does it more frequently in the morning and especially in the mornings when maths appears on the timetable. Joan, who is a chatterbox, is far more of a nuisance when group work is in progress. Such patterns will show themselves in the records of our observations.

Record-keeping, then, is fundamental to the behavioural approach to teaching. Rigorous data collection is essential for scientific research (some examples of which are included as demonstration examples in Part Two of this book) but in every-day classroom teaching we might accept the bare minimum of data collected in the simplest way possible. We now turn to simple methods of observing and recording behaviours which have already been pinpointed because you regard them as important. Simple schedules for observation will be presented to enable you to sample behaviours without taking up too much of your teaching time.

Once you have decided which particular behaviours you are interested in and have pinpointed them accurately you are in a position to begin to observe them. In arriving at exact definitions such as those needed to pinpoint behaviours we sometimes have to be quite arbitrary. For instance, if it is 'calling out' behaviour which we are interested in we may define it as 'Words spoken by Harry which can be heard by the teacher at times when he is supposed to be quiet'. Whether the words can be heard by the teacher or not will depend upon the general noise level in the classroom at the time and so the definition is arbitrary at this point. However, in the observation of behaviour it is objectivity that we are seeking. This means that what you would record as 'calling out' behaviour in this particular set of circumstances would have been observed as such by anyone standing where you were standing and that this same item of behaviour would have been recorded as such by you whether it occurred yesterday, today, or tomorrow. Basically, it is consistency that we are concerned to establish but at the same time we must ensure that the behaviour we have pinpointed is, in fact, relevant to the problem that we are tackling. It is no use applying the ointment to the wrong wound.

Some behaviours are self-recording. Window-breaking leaves pretty obvious results. Most academic behaviours are self-recording in terms of words written or sums completed, whilst even learning material by heart or the learning of principles can be tested quite easily. Social behaviours are, however, usually relatively short-lived and leave no trace, so they have to be observed and noted at the time they occur. In situations where all the behaviour occurring is thought to be important it can be picked up continuously by using a tape-recorder (if it is audible), a video-recorder, or a film. The trouble with such continuous methods is that once you have recorded them they need careful editing and transcribing so that you can then decide which aspects you are interested in. In the classroom we shall seldom be interested in all the behaviour occurring. We can usually decide in advance what behaviour we are interested in and we shall probably be satisfied with a sample. There are practical limits to the amount of information you can process even if your sole task is to observe. You, as a teacher, will have very limited time for observation since you will have to pay attention to other happenings in the classroom at the same time and so a sample will have to suffice. In practical terms you will want to observe and record as little as it is possible to manage with.

It is possible to observe several behaviours at the same time but you are probably going to be concerned with only one or two. Some behaviours like shouting out, banging things about or knocking chairs over are instantaneous and can be tallied over a set period of time. This is called event sampling (see Table 3.1).

In the example given above you would make a point of observing Peter's 'calling out' behaviour for the first five minutes of every half hour when the children were in their seats and working at maths, English, or whatever. During the first period of the week you could put a small pencilled dot in the rectangle under 1 for Monday every time you heard Peter's voice speaking without permission. At the end of five minutes you would add up these dots and enter, say, 6 in the same box. You would do the same for the first five minutes of each half-hour period, as often as you were able during the day. At the end of the week you would have a sample of Peter's 'calling out' behaviour which you plan to change. Some teachers might prefer to tally their observations on a separate piece of paper and enter the numbers on the schedule at the end of the morning. In this case tallying is most easily done by drawing five-bar gates, like this:

$$\text{++++} \; ||| = 8$$

where each line represents an event. If you have access to a tally-counter this task is made even simpler.

The five-minute periods for which you are going to observe must be decided in advance, as in the above example. If you simply wait until you have a quiet spell and choose to do it then because it would be relatively easy, your sample will not be random and representative. You may be in danger of underestimating the extent of your problem. The reason why we need this data is so that once we begin any intervention strategy we can monitor its effects directly and so determine its effectiveness. We shall come back to the details of this process later.

Other behaviours like being out of seat or being on-task, that is, getting on with set work, may be thought of in terms of duration, that is, how long they last. Here we need to employ a different method of recording: a cumulative time-count of seconds or minutes spent, say, working or wandering around. However, this can be very time-consuming even if you have a watch which gives a

Table 3.1 *Event Sampling Schedule*

Session	a.m. 1	2	3	4	5	6	7	8	Total	p.m. 1	2	3	4	5	6	7	8	Total
Monday																		
Tuesday																		
Wednesday																		
Thursday																		
Friday																		

Behaviour to be observed – calling out behaviour.

Pinpointed definition – words spoken by Peter which I can distinguish as his, except when he has been given leave to speak.

Observation method – for the first five minutes of each half-hour period of in-seat work, to be judged by the hands of the classroom clock. Every occurrence to be tallied.

Table 3.2 *Time Sampling Schedule I*

Session	a.m. 1	2	3	4	5	6	7	8	9	10	11	12	p.m. 1	2	3	4	5	6	7	8	9	10	11	12
Monday																								
Tuesday																								
Wednesday																								
Thursday																								
Friday																								

Behaviour to be observed – out of seat behaviour.

Pinpointed definition – child's bottom to be in contact with his *own* seat.

Observation method – once work has been set and children have started to work, an observation will be made at five-minute intervals at the instant that the second (sweep) hand of the clock reaches the vertical position. A tick will be put in the appropriate space if the child is out of seat, otherwise a dash will be put.

cumulative time-count, because you have to be able to note when each occurrence of the behaviour begins and ends. You could, instead, plan to observe your subject for the first five minutes of every hour and count the number of times he gets up out of his seat as in event sampling. (A tally-counter would be useful here.) Alternatively, you might decide to observe him for a set period of time during which you look at him on the instant when the sweep hand of your watch or of a clock passes the vertical position, to observe whether the behaviour is occurring or not (see Table 3.2).

Using a time sampling schedule like the one in Table 3.2 it would be possible at the end of a session to say that nine observations had been made and that on four of these the child was observed to be out of his seat. The same sort of schedule could be used to observe the 'out of seat' behaviour of a group or of a whole class of children. In this case it would be necessary to record, for each observation, how many of the children were out of their seats according to the definition and to enter that number in the appropriate space.

It is difficult to remember to watch the clock in order to take your observation at the exact moment that the second hand passes the vertical position. A better method is to have an audible signal to cue your observation. This then becomes an automatic reminder. A signal can be placed on a cassette quite easily and then played back to give the cue. It is best if the signal can be arranged to come at irregular intervals, but on average, say, once every five minutes. This would give twelve such signals to the hour, with irregular intervals in between. This element of randomness will give a more reliable sample of the behaviour you are observing. Again, it is best if the signal can reach you privately, that is, without the children hearing it also. This can be arranged by using an ear-piece but this may cut down on your mobility unless you have a player that can fit into your pocket. Some teachers have found that their children soon get used to a signal that everyone can hear. The children ignore it after a while.

Once you have learned to observe the behaviour accurately you have to be able to record it immediately and for this a prepared schedule is vital. It does not have to be elaborate but it is best if it bears the pinpointed definition of the behaviour which is being observed and spaces already prepared for tally marks or scores. Two examples have already been given. Another is given in Table 3.3.

Table 3.3 *Time Sampling Schedule II*

Cue		Number of children on-task
		1 2 3 4 5 6 7 8 9 10 11 12 13 14 15 16 17 18 19 20 21 22 23 24
Mon	a.m.	
	p.m.	
Tues	a.m.	
	p.m.	
Wed	a.m.	
	p.m.	
Thurs	a.m.	
	p.m.	
Fri	a.m.	
	p.m.	

Behaviour to be observed – on-task behaviour.
Pinpointed definition – child's eyes to be on paper or book and/or hands to be engaged in writing, cutting, drawing, colouring, sharpening pencil, etc.
Observation method – a cassette-recording will give a signal every sixty seconds. The score will be the number of children on table A who are on-task at that moment.

Using a schedule like the one in Table 3.3 you would be able to get on with whatever you would normally be doing until the cue was heard. Then you would have to look at the table designated and decide how many of the children were on-task according to the definition. If you were interested in the behaviour of the children at one table only, this would be simple enough. If you were interested in the on-task behaviour of the whole class you would have to arrange to observe each of the tables in the classroom in some sort of order, preferably a random one. On this schedule the definition is there to remind you what you are looking for. Initially, it is a good idea to read it over before you start to observe until you are thoroughly at home with the procedure. The idea of the schedule, which may seem to you unduly complicated, is to make the task of observing as easy as possible at the time. The ones given here are meant to be models and to contain all the help you are likely to need but they are not intended to be copied slavishly. You may well be able to get the information you want without anything like this amount of formality. The models are meant to spell out the message that the more you prepare beforehand the less you have to do at the time, and this is an important consideration for the teacher/observer.

Students and teachers who have been able to learn these techniques and to use them in the classroom have expressed amazement at what they have learned about the children. Often they find that the recorded behaviour of the children they are particularly interested in is quite different from what they had supposed. Decisions about what to do, if anything, can then be based upon fact, not conjecture. This is very important.

Observing whilst you are teaching is difficult – perhaps the most difficult technique we are trying to teach in this book, but you will certainly improve with practice. It will become easier and easier as time goes on until it almost becomes second nature. It will enable you to become an efficient and conscious observer of the specific behaviours in which you are really interested and give you accurate information about the children's responses to the material that you are providing for them. It is not always as straightforward as this, however. Some behaviours will occur only in certain situations so that it is useless to attempt to observe them except when the relevant setting events are present. If a child calls out to you only during oral lessons it will be pointless to observe him for this behaviour during a written exercise. Since behaviours, as we have already pointed out, are learned in particular situations, it is in those situations that they are to be found. It is not much use looking for them elsewhere.

Sometimes, the child whose behaviour we are trying to control is just as interested in the process as we are ourselves and he can sometimes be involved in the actual process of recording his own behaviour, as we shall discuss in Chapter 5. With some behaviours which are, at least in part, covert, the person himself may be the only one aware of some instances of the behaviour occurring. This applies to actions like thumb-sucking, which can be carried out surreptitiously. A number of studies have shown instances of children recording their own behaviours once they have been told exactly what has to be done. This is done in school already with academic output where children are encouraged to keep graphical or other records of some of their marks. It can be extended to behaviours like getting out of seat and being on-task, in the right circumstances. There is at least one example in Part Two of this book. Sometimes children can even be involved in observing the behaviour of others, but this needs great care in application.

If you find systematic observation day by day just too much you may instead resort to *probes*. This is where the observer, through lack of time or opportunity, has to be content to sample the rate or level of occurrence of pinpointed behaviours at infrequent intervals and for short periods. Instead of a regular baseline, a few data points are obtained and later on a few more are added. If this is done at the various stages of the exercise it will provide a rudimentary account of what went on and the effects of the various changes that were tried out.

Really good observation techniques are the backbone of the behavioural approach to teaching. They form the basis of sound analysis and effective intervention and give substance to realistic evaluation of what has been achieved. Nevertheless, observation is far from easy and many will find it hard to produce good data. Following the changes recorded in your data will potentially provide your positive reinforcement. Seeing the manifest effects of your intervention in the data you are recording is the best reward of all.

EXERCISES

Attempt these exercises by writing your solutions on a piece of paper before looking at the suggestions given. Remember that we are focusing on B (behaviour) in our ABC model but also that circumstances alter cases. Your solutions may well be better than ours, provided that you can justify them in behavioural terms.

1. What would you pinpoint in the following cases?

Case (*a*)   Not getting on with work
Gerald, aged 10, never does more than a couple of sums or two to three lines of writing in twenty to thirty minutes of working time.
Case (*b*)   Talking
Here we can envisage two problems: Tracey, who hardly ever speaks at all in class even when you, the class teacher, go right up to her; and George who hardly ever *stops* talking, so that you seem to hear him all the time.
Case (*c*)   Attention-seeking
Mary, aged 8, is one of those children who always has to be noticed. When the class are given some work to do she is constantly bringing her work to show you and to get reassurance that she is doing it correctly.

2. Which of these definitions of behaviour is objective enough to be of use in pinpointing? (Would you be able to observe and count the behavioural events as they are defined?)

(*a*)   Making a fuss.
(*b*)   Looking away from the book or paper.
(*c*)   Failure to obey or acknowledge an audible order or summons with five seconds.
(*d*)   Being a nuisance to the teacher or to other children in the room.
(*e*)   The child's bottom being out of contact with the seat of his own chair for more than three seconds.
(*f*)   Getting on with his work and minding his own business.
(*g*)   Bullying behaviour towards smaller children.
(*h*)   Making a noise loud enough to be heard by the teacher above the general noise of the classroom.
(*i*)   Getting out of his seat and causing trouble.
(*j*)   Being untidy.

3. A teacher has decided to count the number of naughty children in her class over a week by putting a tally mark on a sheet whenever she sees a child behaving badly. At the end of the week she summarises her results in a table like this. Use the information

contained in this chapter to comment upon the teacher's attempt to collect data.

	Morning	Afternoon
Monday	26	18
Tuesday	44	39
Wednesday	26	18
Thursday	66	54
Friday	70	20

Chapter 4

Reward and Punishment

The behavioural approach to teaching, as we saw in the overview presented in Chapter 2, is based firmly in the systematic and consistent use of the various forms of reward and, where necessary, punishment available to teachers in the classroom. This is what we mean by consequences, the C in our ABC model. Before detailing specific interventional techniques to bring about changes in children's behaviour, which we will present in the following chapter, it is first necessary to discuss both in more detailed and in more general terms various aspects and issues concerning the use of reward and punishment.

First, however, we wish to put forward and stress the very broad field of application of the behavioural approach in the classroom. It is not to be thought of as the last resort for a weak teacher at his/her wit's end nor the last desperate throw in the reform of some dissolute character. Expert, experienced, successful teachers can use the behavioural approach with profit to their own and their pupils' benefit. Teachers enjoying moderate success can use it to improve their performance and undoubtedly, in the process, both they and their pupils will enjoy their work more. A weaker teacher, prepared to recognise that he/she has a problem and to come to terms with it, can especially benefit. But for all who wish to use it the behavioural approach calls for effort. What each person has to decide is whether the pay-off is worth the effort called for. This is, at the same time, the underlying principle of the whole approach, as will be made clear.

Although we have been writing about the behavioural approach we are not concerned solely with bad behaviour in the sense of the child who is disruptive, naughty, ill-disciplined, or wicked. We *are* concerned with troublesome behaviour of this sort, which we would prefer to call maladaptive, in a particular situation, but we are much more concerned with the establishment and maintenance of acceptable, adaptive, productive repertoires of behaviour, appropriate for specific social situations. This we would refer to as social behaviour and, as we have said before, this is the main concern of this book. However, in school we are concerned also, and some would say mainly, with academic behaviours such as the study skills of attending, responding appropriately, patient exercise of skills, application, and so on. Beyond these instrumental behaviours which contribute to the learning of skills and the accumulation of information we might be led to consider issues like the development of attitudes and the establishment of values. In all of these the behavioural approach has relevance. The behavioural approach can be applied to problems of academic behaviour at all levels and to aspects of both quality and quantity.

Many of the early applications of the behavioural approach were directed towards individuals. In cases of severe disturbance where a very close behavioural analysis and co-ordinated treatment is necessary this may be the only way. Perhaps even in the classroom where one particular child warrants it, individual analysis and treatment may be necessary, but interventions do not have to follow this pattern. Teachers are busy people and are well aware of 'the other twenty-nine' and there is no reason at all why programmes cannot be prepared for small groups, perhaps with individual variations within them. Some programmes have been devised specifically for small groups with a degree of competition between them whilst others operate best by involving the whole class. The behavioural approach is not a rigid system of procedures for certain specific problem cases but a flexible, adaptable approach for analysing and solving a wide range of difficulties encountered by classroom teachers. It helps teachers to make their teaching more effective in all spheres of their classroom practice.

BEHAVIOURAL DEFINITIONS OF REWARD AND
PUNISHMENT

So far in this book we have used the terms reward and punishment fairly loosely and as if their meanings were self-evident and their effects upon behaviour obvious. However, there is one major snag. This may be summed up by quoting the old adage 'One man's meat is another man's poison'. In other words, what is rewarding for me may not be a reward for you. It would obviously be ineffective to give a record by Frank Sinatra, a performer you greatly admire, to an adolescent who is 'into punk rock'. On the other hand, whilst most of us would find being told off aversive we have seen that some children will be reinforced by the attention they get from being reprimanded, since it is better than no attention at all. This was certainly true of the children watched by Jan in the railway carriage in Chapter 1.

All of this leads us to an important behavioural distinction. We do not define punishers or reinforcers. They define themselves by their effects on behaviour. Thus behavioural psychologists have developed a convention whereby reinforcers are defined as only those consequences which, when following a behaviour, increase the likelihood of its being repeated. Attention may be a positive reinforcer to one person, an aversive consequence to another. Similarly, the term punisher is defined empirically and according to the observed consequences. If it is a consequence of the behaviour and that behaviour subsequently tends to be repeated less often, then that consequence may be referred to as a punisher.

WHAT IS REINFORCING?

As mentioned earlier, a key underlying principle of the behavioural approach is finding out what people will 'go for', that is, what they find reinforcing. This will vary from situation to situation, from person to person and from time to time, but not all that much. In behavioural terms reinforcement is defined pragmatically. Whatever proves to be a consistent, immediate and contingent consequence of a response and which at the same time brings about an increase in the rate of the response is a positive reinforcer. For most people most of the time we can be fairly sure what things will be positively reinforcing. Giving people things to eat and drink or things to wear are reinforcing. These are called primary reinforcers because they are necessary, in the last resort, for the survival of the species. Likewise, adults and most children have learned to respond to social signals like smiling, compliments and other gestures of approval and acceptance from the people around them. Such gestures become reinforcing through being associated with primary reinforcers on a number of occasions in the first place and are regarded as secondary reinforcers.

Some reinforcers, of which money is the best example, owe their reinforcing power to the fact that they give free access to other things which are themselves reinforcing. Such reinforcers are called *tokens* and their great advantage is that they make it possible to reinforce immediately in situations where the handing out of primary reinforcers would be difficult. This situation frequently obtains in school and hence marks, stars and points are often used as tokens. It is important to point out, however, that initially token reinforcers should be directly linked to established reinforcers. Such *back-up* reinforcers might take the form of preferred activities, for example, which are made contingent upon amassing a certain number of points or tokens. Avril will be allowed the privilege of feeding the guinea pig for the following week when she has collected ten points for punctual attendance. Teachers have a whole range of such activities at their disposal for use as back-up reinforcers. Moreover, tokens frequently acquire power in their own right, through association with back-up reinforcers, so that eventually children work for tokens alone or for tokens which are only backed up by yet more tokens, for example, badges, certificates, cups, and so on.

Another useful distinction can be made between intrinsic consequences and extrinsic ones. Intrinsic consequences are those changes which are brought about by (and are dependent upon) the behaviour of the individual who experiences them. Since personal experience is really beyond the brief of a truly behavioural description we shall have to be content to say that intrinsic reinforcement takes the form of feelings of satisfaction (with a job well done, for example) or pleasure associated with the behaviour itself (for example, the vicarious experiences accompanying reading). Such consequences may be contrasted with extrinsic consequences which are provided by (and dependent upon) the behaviour of others. It is this second class of consequences which lends itself so well to manipulation and which is the basis of so many behavioural interventions.

In the last analysis, as has already been stated, what a person will 'go for' is a matter for experiment. Teachers are especially fortunate in that the classroom and the school contain a great many objects and events which are reinforcing for children. These vary from acting as a monitor to writing on the blackboard, using certain apparatus, having free time to choose an activity, being read to, playing games, and so on. One way to establish the currency of these activities is to observe the children. Another is simply to ask them what they like to do. In some programmes arranged by teachers a menu of such activities is exhibited. Used in a behavioural context with clearly defined and positive criteria, quite ordinary events of the school routine can be used by a skilful teacher to improve some aspects of class behaviour. For example, by giving the opportunity of using the last few minutes of the physical education lesson for a game popular with the children, certain aspects of the class routine such as registration or getting down to work on a written exercise could be improved. This is where the skilled and imaginative teacher can apply behavioural methods to good effect. Activities and events which seem quite banal to adults have proved to be very effective as reinforcers in the school situation.

Another useful technique to be borne in mind is the Premack principle or, to give it a more homely title, 'Grandma's law'. Grandma's law, simply stated, is 'You can have your pudding when you have eaten up all your vegetables'. Note the constructive and positive form in which this has been put; the negative has purposely been avoided. Premack's principle states more formally that high probability behaviour (eating pudding) can be used to reinforce low probability behaviour (eating up all your vegetables) when the first is made dependent upon the second. Taken to its logical conclusion, anything that a person does not like doing can be reinforced by making something that he does like doing dependent upon it.

Let us take a specific example. A teacher identified a boy who had a problem with his maths. It was not that he *could not* do the exercise, he just *did not*! He would find all sorts of reasons for not getting on with his work; when he did work, he did so very slowly and untidily, making many careless errors. The teacher also knew that this boy loved to write stories. She obtained a very good quality exercise-book with stiffened covers quite different from the normal school books and wrote his name on the outside so that it looked very attractive. She then gave him his maths exercise to do, making sure that it was well within his capability, and said, 'When you bring me your exercise of ten examples neatly completed you can have this book (the new exercise book) and write me a story'. In twenty-five minutes he presented his completed maths paper – the first time he had ever completed an exercise. Unfortunately the teacher had made a mistake in this programme for her problem now became one of getting the boy to stop writing and to do anything else. She should have put a limit from the outset on the length of time for which he would be allowed to write; twenty minutes would have been reasonable. Apart from this we have a very good example of Premack's principle in practice and a very simple and successful intervention.

Before we go on to summarise the main points of how to use reinforcers effectively there is another important issue to consider. Once we have introduced an intervention employing extrinsic reinforcers, the child will begin to behave differently. If we now remove these new consequences, then, according to our theory, we would expect the child's behaviour to revert to what it was before the intervention. The trick is to find a way of bringing the new behaviour under the control first of more naturally occurring reinforcers and eventually of intrinsic reinforcers. This is a crucial weaning process which depends on the recognition and understanding of two important factors: first, that there is a *hierarchy of reinforcers*, and second, that the effects of a reinforcer depend upon the *schedule of reinforcement* under which it is applied. Let us take these one at a time.

Hierarchy of Reinforcers

Some responses we make habitually; some we make willingly with little incentive; whilst some we feel that we would never do. But, as the saying goes, 'Everyone has his price', and certainly each of us has a, probably unconscious, gradient of reinforcement. We would be prepared to act in a certain way if it were made worth our while. By and large primary reinforcers, especially where prior deprivation is severe, are the most powerful. What would a person dying of thirst not promise to do for a drink of water? Tokens giving access to primary or conditioned reinforcers will also be powerful. Few members of our society will not respond to offers of money, the generalised token which gives access to all goods and services. Moreover, since man is a social animal he learns to respond to social reinforcement since, to most of us, the good opinion of our fellows means a great deal. Lastly, there is the intrinsic group of reinforcers referred to earlier. If we bring about change through use of one of the stronger, extrinsic group of reinforcers, then we must arrange that the control is passed, by degrees, to social and finally to intrinsic reinforcers so that when the extrinsic reinforcement is withdrawn the desired behaviour will continue. Here, the importance of gradualness cannot be overstressed, neither can the importance of linking the use of primary and token reinforcers with social reinforcement all along the line. Behaviour which clearly meets with approval from significant others (that is, people who are important in a child's life) will be maintained and this provides a bridge to eventual control by intrinsic reinforcement.

Schedules of Reinforcement

When a new behaviour is being learned it is necessary that the positively reinforcing consequence should be immediately apparent and should be applied in abundance, *every time* that the desired behaviour occurs. As the rate of responding increases the consequences can be applied at a 'leaner' rate and even a small time-lapse may be tolerated between the response and the reinforcer. Once again, changes must be introduced gradually whilst the continuing process of monitoring provides a check throughout. Eventually, the high rate of responding can be maintained by intermittent application of the consequences with greater and greater delays. Experiments have shown clearly that behaviours maintained on such schedules are extremely resistant to *extinction*. Extinction refers to the process whereby behaviours which are not followed by a positive consequence gradually decrease in frequency and eventually cease.

USING REINFORCERS EFFECTIVELY

We now know the sorts of things which children will typically find reinforcing but this is not enough. To increase behaviour, we must provide new, positive consequences but we must also do it *systematically*. A number of ground rules come into operation here and these are:

(1) The consequences must be applied contingently and only contingently. In other words, whatever consequences are to be applied must be linked clearly and inevitably to the behaviour we are concerned with. Clear definition of particular behaviours was stressed in Chapter 3 and this is because we, teachers or parents, as well as the child himself, have to know exactly what behaviour we are concerned to change so that we can reinforce contingently and accurately.

(2) The consequences must be evident as soon as possible after the behaviour occurs. There must be a minimum of delay since this weakens the effect. This is why tokens are

sometimes used since they can be given immediately following appropriate behaviour and 'cashed in' at a later time.

(3) The consequences must be applied with absolute consistency like the natural consequences of some physical acts. For example, if you touch the glowing element of an electric fire you will be burned. If you touch it a second time it will burn you again even if this time you do it unwittingly. That is consistency. Inconsistent use of reinforcement leads to a confused child who will not know how he is supposed to behave.

(4) In the early stages of unlearning or of learning new behaviours results will come sooner if the consequences are applied in abundance. At a later stage the level of the 'pay-off' can be reduced, and indeed, the maintenance of a high level of responding, once established, will be enhanced if the reinforcement only comes intermittently.

This heavy emphasis on precision gives the impression that the behavioural approach is a very cold, clinical business but in practice this is far from being the case. As we have said, social reinforcement in the form of discernible genuine, human warmth and caring should always accompany other forms of reinforcement since this is what maintains our behaviour in the real world. There is a sense in which a behavioural intervention has to be mechanical, automatic, remote and impersonal. This is unlike many disciplinary regimes, especially those between parents and children within a family, where a mother may imply that by behaving in certain ways the children are letting her down, disappointing or even humiliating her. To act in this way is a form of moral blackmail and is likely to make for further trouble in the family. The behavioural approach is different in that whilst the regime may appear to be mechanical, it is applied to the behaviour, not the person. We recognise the act as inappropriate, disruptive, or naughty, *not* the person. The natural emotional response of the parent towards the child can be channelled in his encounter with the rule structure. In just the same way that a child can be comforted if his encounter with the natural world produces a burned finger or a grazed knee, so we can commiserate with the child who fails to meet certain criteria of behaviour. The fact that we know and the child knows that fire burns does not prevent us from being sympathetic and helpful when an accident occurs. So, too, we can be sympathetic towards the child who fails to meet some behavioural target and give encouragement for better outcomes in the future.

Before moving on to consider the applications of positive reinforcement, and other aspects of the behavioural approach, in actual classroom teaching, let us consider the more traditional form of achieving classroom discipline, punishment.

WHY NOT USE PUNISHMENT?

By punishment we mean the presentation of an aversive event following the occurrence of a behaviour which has the effect of reducing the frequency of occurrence of that behaviour. Advocates of the behavioural approach to teaching object to the use of punishment, not because of ethical or moral considerations (which they may also hold), but simply because punitive techniques are, in the long run, ineffective. Punished behaviour is merely temporarily suppressed and is likely to recur once the punishment or fear of punishment is removed. Consequently, one needs to continue punishing to suppress a behaviour over a period of time and the mere fact of repeating the punishment is likely to lessen its effectiveness, possibly precipitating the escalation to more severe forms.

Many schools still seem to be based on the principle of punishing unwanted behaviours whether those behaviours are failures to learn or antisocial acts. School rules invariably consist of a list of 'thou shalt nots', whilst appropriate behaviour is expected rather than encouraged and is rarely specified. Infractions of school rules are commonly punished, not only physically but by children being verbally abused, sarcastically scored off, shown up in front of peers and generally demeaned. None of this is conducive to learning appropriate behaviours but will result only in forms of *escape/avoidance behaviours* which may sometimes include doing what the teacher wants but may more frequently include opting out of his area of influence whenever possible.

Why then do parents and teachers continue to use punishment since it is so ineffective and has so many drawbacks? One possibility is that they continue to punish because occasionally, in the past, punishing the child has led to the immediate (but temporary) cessation of an unwanted behaviour. In so far as this reinforces the adult (she got what she wanted) she will continue to indulge in punishing behaviour even though she is only occasionally reinforced by its having the desired effect. In other words, the adult's behaviour is under the control of an intermittent schedule of reinforcement – one of the most powerful means of maintaining a behaviour and highly resistant to extinction. The adult and child are thus, literally, in a vicious circle.

We might add that an adult who is associated with punishment in the eyes of a child becomes a person to be avoided or escaped from and so becomes less effective as a 'rewarder'. Reinforcing is easy when the relationship is close and positive. The mutual rewarding between lovers is such that the mere presence of the other person is sufficient reinforcement. To many older children, in particular, teachers who continually reprimand, criticise and forbid rapidly lose any value as potential sources of reinforcement.

In the last resort punishment teaches children that might is right. A child who is physically punished for errors or for mis-demeanours can easily learn to adopt the same tactics with his juniors and may justify his bullying by suggesting that adults punish him for doing things that they disapprove of and that he is applying the same principle to those that get in his way.

A moment's thought reveals the nonsense of attempting to teach by means of punishment. Consider a simple learning situation where the teacher wants the child, Gavin, to get on with his work ('studying behaviour') and not to chatter, not to look out of the window, not to get out of his seat, not to disturb other children, and so on. Remembering that punishment constitutes an attempt to eliminate a certain behaviour by making aversive consequences contingent upon that behaviour, the teacher decides to punish Gavin whenever he does anything other than get on with his work. She decides to deliver a very definite punisher and smack him when he engages in anything other than studying behaviour. Gavin pinches his neighbour, she smacks him. He gets up, she smacks him again. He looks out of the window, she smacks him again, harder this time. He begins to wail, she smacks him again. Gavin wails louder than ever; the teacher feels exhausted and miserable. All of her attention has been focused on only one child, ignoring the other twenty-nine who are now all watching her and Gavin, and still she has failed to teach him to get on with his work. All of this points to the simple fact that it is far more efficient to reinforce desired behaviour than it is to punish all the unwanted behaviours: for example, by remarking, 'Look how well Gavin is getting on with his work'.

Delivering punishment also has another danger, as we

mentioned earlier: it paves the way for shaping up other unwanted behaviour by means of negative reinforcement. By definition, we do not like or 'go for' punishment and we attempt to avoid it. Consequently, avoiding the teacher, running out of the class, or staying away from school are behaviours which will be rapidly learned if the child is continually punished in school, as they constitute an escape from punishment and are hence (negatively) reinforcing. It seems reasonable to suggest that such behaviour may often be simply the product of a school environment which the child finds either aversive or lacking in positive reinforcements compared with what is available outside. The behavioural teacher would argue that in order to be successful, schools must be places where the desired behaviours are carefully specified and positive reinforcement is made contingent upon them. The main emphasis should be on positive reinforcement in order to maintain an efficient and effective learning situation and which will, as a result, also be a happy one.

EXERCISES

1.   This exercise requires you to count instances of your own normal behaviour in the classroom. Observe yourself for fifteen minutes for each of the two behaviours listed below taking care to time the period accurately and to count every instance of the behaviour. If you have access to a tally-counter it makes the job much easier but you can do it almost as well simply by making a mark on a sheet of paper every time you observe yourself behaving in the way defined. At this stage you should be attempting to observe how you usually behave and you should not be making any attempt to change.

(a)   *Negative teacher behaviours.* Count each instance that you respond negatively to an individual child or the class as a whole. Remember negative responses are not only verbal but can be gestural, postural, or conveyed by facial expression.

(b)   *Positive teacher behaviours.* This time count each instance of your positive reponses to children in your class. Again they may be conveyed verbally or non-verbally.

We would suggest that you carry out the exercise above on three or four separate occasions for each behaviour. Once you have collected three or four samples of your usual classroom behaviour, you could attempt to change it and monitor your success by continuing to observe yourself. Attempt to reduce your use of negative comments, gestures, and so on, and, at the same time, increase your rate of positive responses. Your observations will provide you with useful feedback on how well you are progressing if you are able to continue to observe yourself regularly two or three times in each week. It is a good idea to choose similar class activities as occasions for observing yourself and remember to record for fifteen minutes exactly.

The aim of this exercise is to increase your rate of positive behaviours and to decrease the number of negative responses you make. The idea is to 'beat your negatives', that is, to improve your ratio of positive to negative responses.

At this point it is important to reiterate our earlier point about contingencies. The behavioural approach is not about being Mr Nice Guy (or Ms Nice Gal) who continually praises regardless of what is happening; it is about identifying appropriate classroom behaviour and attempting to increase its occurrence by rewarding instances of it.

2.　Make a list of ten remarks which you could make to children who are doing well in order to reinforce their actions positively. Remember that in order to be effective such remarks must:

(*a*)　be positive;
(*b*)　be specific to the desired behaviour;
(*c*)　be appropriate to the age (stage) of the children you teach and to the situation;
(*d*)　feel comfortable and natural for you to use.

3.　Make a list of ten items or activities which are available to you in the classroom and which might be used as positive reinforcers.

Chapter 5

Changing Children's Behaviour

In a sense, all that has gone before in this book is by way of preparation for the present chapter. In Chapter 4 we looked, in some detail, at the general techniques available to us for bringing about behaviour change by manipulating the consequences. In Chapter 3 we discussed the need for careful pinpointing and recording of behaviour in order to find out exactly what is happening in the classroom. We stressed that pinpointing makes the task of observing much easier and more precise since it forces us to count clearly defined events. Counting, recording and analysing the frequency with which behaviours occur is fundamental to the behavioural approach. Later, in Part Two, we will consider this in greater detail and suggest ways in which your observation records can be summarised so that you can see at a glance what is going on. We are now in a position to put the A, B and C back together again. Here, we hope to demonstrate how behaviour can be analysed and, if necessary, a strategy developed to bring about a change.

CHANGING BEHAVIOUR BY CHANGING THE ANTECEDENTS

A glance back to Chapter 2 will remind you of the ABC model in which we spelled out the relationship between antecedents and behaviours. It has been shown clearly that a change in the antecedents, by itself, can bring about desired changes in behaviour. One example of this is the use of 'carrels'. Some children (often called hyperactive) are stimulated to noisy behaviour by the presence of other children around them. If they are placed in a small work area screened off from the other children but still in the same room (that is, in a carrel) they are able to concentrate for quite long periods and do satisfactory work. Again, it has been shown experimentally that, although it has been thought by some that grouping children around a nest of tables produces co-operation and other social rewards, it also produces a lot of chatter between the members of the group. If Harry talks to Susan across the tables then Jean, Mary, Syd and John all become involved. If the class are sitting in rows there is far less talking and if neighbours do chat they do not automatically involve the others. Where concentration upon a private task is the object, sitting in rows would seem to have in-built advantages. (See Classroom Demonstration Study 15 in Chapter 8 for a fuller description.)

All of us behave in different ways in different settings. Compare your own behaviour in the headteacher's room, in the staffroom and in your own classroom. Think how you behave at a concert, at a political meeting and in a restaurant. Much can be done by ensuring that children know the rules for behaving in different situations and by being consistent. At one time schools used to have clear rules for behaviour in certain places like corridors, stairs, and so on. If we have none at all, some children find the situation confusing in that they do not know what behaviour is appropriate and what is expected of them. A lot of the behaviour of children which parents and teachers find annoying arises because there is no agreement about what kinds of behaviour are appropriate and acceptable in given situations. An example, a real one, will illustrate. A little girl was observed standing with her mother in a queue in a very busy post office just before Christmas. The child remained near her mother but was jigging up and down, sometimes skipping a few yards away. This was obviously upsetting the mother because she kept grasping the child's arm to keep her by her side. When the child inquired, 'Are we going to see Granny after this?', she replied, 'I shall not take you at all if you are naughty'. This is a clear case of a mis-match in the definition of what is acceptable behaviour. The mother thought that the child's behaviour was inappropriate although nobody else around seemed to notice what the child was doing or to be upset by it, nor was the child made aware of what was 'naughty' about her behaviour. This sort of thing can happen in the school situation too. There, however, the other children will often transmit rule expectations to their peers but this may not happen with the isolated, renegade type of child, which is one reason why he tends to be involved so frequently in confrontations with authority. Adults do children no favours, however, when they fail to spell out the rules for appropriate behaviour.

CHANGING BEHAVIOUR BY CHANGING THE CONSEQUENCES

It is not always possible to change a behaviour by changing the situation in which it occurs. Moreover, children, as we have said, have to learn what are the appropriate behaviours for a given situation, and the way in which they learn these is as a result of the consequences following their behaviour in different situations. In the ABC model, C, the consequences, describe what happens to the child after the behaviour occurs. Systematically altering the consequences is the most powerful and most direct method of changing behaviour. We have set out the theoretical position on rewarding and punishing events in Chapter 2 and in Chapter 4 we discussed the effects of positive consequences in some detail. We shall be developing these ideas in the following sections and other examples will be found in Part Two of this book.

CATEGORIES OF BEHAVIOUR TO BE CHANGED

We will assume that having looked at a child's behaviour in the classroom context we can justify an attempt to change it in relation to one or more of the three criteria outlined in Chapter 3. Before we decide which strategy to adopt it is important to classify behaviour change into three broad categories. We need to decide whether:

(1) there is a deficit in behaviour, that is, the desired behaviour never occurs at all;
(2) the behaviour is acceptable but does not occur often enough; or
(3) the behaviour is unacceptable and we wish to reduce it or eliminate its occurrence altogether.

So our problem may be one of teaching a completely new behaviour, encouraging wanted behaviours, or eliminating certain other, unwanted behaviours. Another way of putting this would be to say that some behaviours we wish to increase and some we wish to decrease and that for each of these the behavioural approach has a different remedy.

(1) TEACHING NEW BEHAVIOUR

In this section we are assuming that we have a complete deficit in the behavioural repertoire. We have a child who is completely lacking in some social skill. For example, Susan never contributes to class discussion, whilst Charlie never says 'Thank you'. This really is the basic problem of teaching: producing a behaviour where none existed before.

Shaping

If we wait passively for the behaviour to occur in order to apply reinforcement then we shall wait for ever. Somehow, we have got to arrange for the behaviour to occur: *to make it occur* if need be. However, if we expect a perfect example of the behaviour from the child before reinforcing him, then we shall fail. What we have to do is to apply the technique known as *shaping* or, more technically, as *successive approximations*. In using this technique we begin to apply positive reinforcement to any response which begins to approach, by however small a degree, the final behaviour we have in mind. For example, the first stage in getting Charlie to say 'Thank you' would be to establish eye-contact at the moment of giving him something. When this has been done we would concentrate on getting him to copy our 'Thank you'. Then we could encourage his 'Thank you' with a smile, withholding the object until his response was complete. Finally, all our prompts and cues would be removed, although praise and encouragement would still be given immediately his response occurred.

Fading

In the example just given we can see two processes in operation. Shaping refers to manipulating the child's responses gradually towards some criterion of performance. *Fading* is the term applied to the gradual reduction of prompts, cues, frequency of reinforcement, and so on. You can see that shaping calls for a great deal of insight, skill and patience. It is necessary to recognise small changes in behaviour that can be used as steps on the way to the final desired outcome and to reinforce these, but not for a period long enough to establish them. We shall constantly be looking for further approximations towards better performance and withholding reinforcement (another aspect of fading) until these are produced. At the same time we have to keep up the rate of reinforcement, otherwise we risk the child losing interest altogether and refusing to co-operate. Generally, with normal children progress is rapid. Working with children who have gross motor or intellectual defects calls for much greater skill and patience and is outside the scope of this book.

Guiding

If we cannot get a child to respond at all we may have to produce the necessary response by *guiding*. This means that the child's limbs are held and pushed or guided through the process. To begin with, the teacher of young children who wants her class to raise their hands when they wish to speak to her may physically lift the arms of individuals, guiding them in the production of the appropriate response. Similarly, parents help their children to hold and swing a cricket bat or to cup their hands to catch a ball.

Prompting

At a later stage guiding may be replaced by *prompting*. When the guided responses are learned so as to require minimal intervention by the teacher or parent then physical contact may no longer be necessary and a cue or prompt substituted. So, for example, the teacher will now merely have to signal with an upward movement of her hand that the children must raise their hands when they wish to speak. Parents may indicate actions by demonstrating the cupping of the hands for the children to copy or they may use a verbal prompt, like 'Hands ready'.

Modelling

Sometimes sub-skills are present but are not being properly sequenced. Here, *modelling* may be the answer. Another child, or an adult for that matter, demonstrates the sequence and the subject is invited to copy. It is easy enough for the teacher to call the attention of her class to an individual social skill which has just been performed expertly. She may comment upon some action, as in 'Look how quietly Ben and Peter are working together and what a lovely rocket they are making'. Some teachers find that to refer to an individual or group who are behaving well at that moment is the best way to bring the whole class to order. They may say something like 'I'm glad to see that red group are ready for the next step'. In other cases it may be necessary to have a skilled child go through the whole process and to draw attention to particular sub-skills and sequences. An example of this might be when teaching young children how to take a message to another member of staff. The whole process may then be acted through with the teacher pointing out the proper mode of address, and so on. At a later stage we might see a similar process being employed when children are being taught to cope with being interviewed or taking an oral or practical examination. Much athletic and other skill training is done in this way by learning sub-skills and then learning and improving sequences. The coach is there to guide and model and then to fade prompts and give positive reinforcement for successful outcomes.

These techniques constitute *real* teaching and *real* learning. Much of what goes on in schools is a matter of presenting a succession of hurdles and providing evidence (results) to show who has jumped over them and who has failed to do so. This process does not teach. As the old saying has it, 'Teaching is not telling'. The teacher's job should be more concerned with structuring the task, arranging for success and providing positive reinforcement until the natural and intrinsic rewards, which come from the mastery of the skill and the completion of the task itself, take over. Once the batsman is scoring centuries he needs no one to tell him how good he is. Once the child is able to read an exciting story she needs no one to urge her to go back to the library. It is at the early stages, when progress is slow and much less obvious, when rewards provided by the natural environment are meagre and hard won, that *real* teaching comes in to provide artificial (extrinsic) rewards for effort and for progress, however small.

(2) INCREASING INFREQUENT BEHAVIOUR

In behavioural terms, to increase the rate at which a certain behaviour occurs we usually have to alter the consequences so as to provide outcomes that are consistent and more positively reinforcing. If a child is able to work quietly but does not do so very often we could say that the consequences which follow his working quietly are not sufficiently reinforcing. We can only find out what will reinforce him by experimenting with different consequences and observing their effect on his behaviour. It is possible that the very fact that the teacher begins to pay attention to his quiet behaviour (by commenting favourably upon it) will be reinforcing to the child. He will then be more likely to work quietly in the future.

Sometimes, an increase in the rate of a behaviour can be brought about by changing the circumstances, that is, the setting. The effect of changing seating patterns has already been referred to. Making certain that children know exactly what they are expected to do, where equipment is kept and how and when they are to have access to it, how they are to recognise that the given task is complete and what they are to do next, are all part of the total setting. Children need to know whether interaction with others is permitted or encouraged in particular circumstances. All these, and many other factors which will occur to practising teachers, are part of the setting or the antecedent situation in the classroom. They are all subject to the teacher's manipulation which forms part of his professional competence.

Cueing

A child who can speak quite well but who seldom does so may need *cueing*. This involves signalling, either verbally or non-verbally, appropriate opportunities to the child and encouraging him to try to respond. All his attempts would then be reinforced appropriately. Once he begins to contribute to class discussion at a level comparable with his peers the cues would be faded. Alternatively, we may have a child who very rarely speaks in class through shyness or fear of failure. A quiet word with such a child could establish an agreed private cue to be given when he feels that he has something to contribute. When he uses this you could go up to him to receive an almost private communication. If, and when, you feel it appropriate, this could be exhibited to the rest of the class, not only as the shy child's contribution, but a worthy one at that. By degrees the child could be encouraged to speak more audibly and more often, once he realises that his contribution to the class discussion is accepted and valued by the group as a whole. Finally, he will be able to conform to class custom for taking part generally. Both of these procedures exemplify the basic solution for increasing the rates of infrequent behaviour: to give the response every opportunity to occur and, when it does, to give appropriate positive reinforcement. The last stage is to fade out the extra prompts or other aids.

Social Reinforcement

Adults, especially parents and teachers, who have close contact with them, find that children respond very well to the use of attention and praise. This is called *social reinforcement* and is very effective, especially with young children. On the whole teachers say that they believe in encouraging children by means of praise and attention and they doubtless mean what they say, but we have found in our research that most teachers use social reinforcement much less than they think they do and certainly much less than they could. Of course, some people find it easy to use praise whilst others find it very difficult, but we all do it sometimes and so we could all learn to use praise more frequently and effectively.

This does not mean using praise all the time and whatever the outcomes. When we were speaking to a teacher about this recently he recalled that he had once worked in a school where the headmaster was always praising his staff and that this had resulted in a falling off in effort and in standards. This illustrates very well the point that we are making and which we have already referred to in Chapter 4, that reinforcement must be used *contingently* and *only contingently* to be really effective. If it is to work best, it must also, at the outset at any rate, be immediate and abundant. It is no good waiting until the next day to reinforce a young child in the early stages of increasing a behaviour. Moreover, the more abundant the reinforcement, the more effective it will be, at first, in increasing the frequency of the behaviour.

Now, although we have been stressing throughout the need for accuracy and objectivity in observing and recording, this does not mean that our interactions with the children have to be clinical, scientific and cold. Not a bit of it! A great deal of this work can be fun and would seem like a game to the child. Many of the interventions described in the second part of this book have been enjoyed by the children involved to the extent that they often reminded their teacher of the game they were using to improve some aspect of classroom social behaviour, if he or she forgot.

Rules

By and large, our society recognises the necessity for rules to guide the behaviour of its members and proceeds to write laws and rules to provide a framework. Almost exclusively, however, these rules are framed in negative terms: 'Thou shalt not steal', and so on. Whether it is a matter of dealing truthfully with one's neighbour, rules for the safety and convenience of others, or just a matter of appearances, the result is always the same: rules are inevitably expressed negatively. We are told, 'Do not walk on the grass', or 'Do not touch'. In order to ensure that people keep these rules, society appoints officers like policemen, traffic wardens, museum- and park-keepers. In the last resort, they report misdemeanours and the guilty are punished, probably, as in Voltaire's phrase, 'Pour encourager les autres'. But punishment, by itself, does not teach any alternative acceptable behaviours.

The behavioural approach is contrary to this. Rules are formulated in a way that sets out the behaviour that is desired. That is to say, they are put positively *not* negatively. In the classroom we might have 'We try to work quietly', 'We stay in our seats unless we have permission to move', 'We put up our hands when we have something to say', and so on. We have found that this procedure works better if children are involved and encouraged to generate a set of rules acceptable to teacher and class. (But beware – some of their suggestions can be *very* negative.) The teacher's task is then to ignore any failure to keep the rules, unless someone else is really at risk, to catch the children who are being good (that is, keeping the rules) and to provide positive reinforcement for them contingently, abundantly and immediately. This is a formula which has been used widely in research and has been found to be very effective. We usually refer to it as 'rules, praise and ignoring' and several examples of its use are included in Part Two of this book.

Tokens

A good intervention strategy will give the child an achievable target from the start and will also provide a means by which he can see his progress towards it. One way of doing this is by using *tokens*. These can take the form of any objects or visible marks which are easy to handle and see, but not easy to copy nor readily available from elsewhere. Plastic discs or counters, buttons, draughts pieces, or cards with the official school stamp on them have all been used successfully. Most teachers already use stars, points, order marks, and so on, as rewards, sometimes as part of the school system, so the idea is far from new. Tokens or tallies can be collected and then counted up at set times or they may be fixed to a chart so that they can be clearly seen all the time. The visual display is especially important where there is a target to be achieved, as in the case referred to in the preceding paragraph. As the target is changed so the display can vary also. For example, one teacher used a cardboard cut-out train which was moved along a track towards the station to indicate progress towards a rewarding situation. The track could then be lengthened to accommodate changes in the rewarding strategy.

Tokens have other advantages. They allow us to reward immediately for small incremental changes in behaviour – another aspect of thinking small. Many rewards used in interventions cannot be subdivided into small units. For example, in the classroom the reward could well be a period for using some special apparatus or a chosen activity which involves the rest of the group. The use of tokens allows us to give, as it were, a small portion of the reward immediately for a small unit of behaviour – the sort of unit we shall be observing and recording. In addition, the use of tokens allows us to vary the reward and/or the 'cost' of the reward without the tokens themselves losing currency. Some intervention strategies involve the use of a *token economy* where tokens become the currency for all sorts of privileges and activities throughout the classroom or school. In such situations a tariff or price list is published so that children can see what their tokens will buy. This is mentioned by way of illustration only, since we are not advocating token economies for normal schools. Such a powerful (and complicated) procedure can seldom be justified as strictly necessary although tokens can be used in ordinary classrooms in a number of ways. They are very useful in that they provide a visual aid at the beginning of a programme and a ready means for fading the programme once behaviour change has been achieved. Examples of the use of tokens will be found in Part Two of this book.

Contracting

Contracting can be a very powerful device, especially with older children who have a problem (whether behavioural or academic), are aware of it and who want help in solving it. Contracts are based upon the same principles as other interventions. Early goals must be realisable. Criteria must be defined so that all parties understand exactly what is involved and the consequences must be clearly spelled out. Because of the necessity of changing criteria, reward schedules, and so on, contracts should be made for short periods of a week or so to allow for such revision. They should always be written and formally signed by all the participants. An example might be:

> Each day of the week I, Sidney Jones, will write at least ten lines in my exercise-book. Each line must start within half an inch from the margin and must contain at least six words. For each day that this is done I, Mrs Smith, will give Sidney a star. When Sidney has four stars he will be allowed half an hour on Friday afternoon to use any of the apparatus in the classroom cupboard with the help of any friend he chooses.
>
> *Signed*   Mrs G Smith   Sidney Jones
>   2 April 1981

It should not be forgotten that children are interacting with other adults both in school and outside and that some of the behaviours we are concerned with occur both in and out of school. There is no reason at all why some or all of these people may not be involved in intervention programmes, and contracting is a very good way of bringing them in. Parents, for example, control some very powerful reinforcers for their children at home and they will probably be just as interested as the child's teacher in helping him to progress academically or improve his social behaviour in the school situation. There is no reason why improved behaviour in school should not carry over into the home but it will only do so if similar behavioural strategies are used to control it. Where adults other than the teacher are active in the classroom/school it is essential that they are involved in interventions and given clear instructions, otherwise the consistency so essential to a behavioural programme can be destroyed. For instance, where bullying is a problem, much of it will take place in the playground or in the road outside the school where the co-operation of duty teachers, lunch-hour supervisors and even lollipop people will be necessary.

Self-recording

Again with older children who recognise their problem and who want to do something about it, *self-recording* may be a possibility. This is particularly so when the behaviours are covert, or partly so, like day-dreaming, nail-biting, chewing, or smoking. Quite young children are capable of self-recording the results of academic outcomes like the numbers of spellings they have correct or the number of pages read in a given period. As with all behavioural events, careful objective definition is of great importance. When self-recording is attempted, at least in the early stages, it will probably be necessary to have some means of checking the accuracy of the recording. Self-recording may well lead to greater self-awareness, a recognition of one's own behaviour patterns, and it is a small step from there to self-control through self-reinforcement. Planning to arrange reinforcing events for oneself is not far removed from the joint planning involved in contracting, nor from the self-awareness brought about through self-recording. Logically, perhaps, this is the place for *teachers* to start, since in order to bring about behavioural change in children they have first to change their own behaviour.

At least one teacher began to use behavioural methods by allowing his class of secondary-aged boys to modify his behaviour first. He asked the children which of his behaviours annoyed them the most and found, to his chagrin, that it was his use of sarcasm. He allowed the class to help him to record the incidence of this behaviour and it was agreed with them that if he could reduce it below a certain level by the end of the week, they would reward him by giving him a lesson of complete peace and quiet on the Friday. This was achieved and the success of the demonstration allowed the teacher to begin to use behavioural interventions with his pupils.

(3) REDUCING UNWANTED BEHAVIOUR

So far we have considered only the positive side, that is, of increasing the incidence of desired behaviours, but many teachers are concerned about other behaviours such as tardiness, untidiness, disobedience, stealing and disruptive acts which they want to decrease. It is to these that we now turn. The reaction of most adults to behaviours like these would be to use punishment of some sort. But, as we discussed in the last chapter, the use of punishment carries with it the risk of a number of unwanted side-effects and, anyway, it is not very effective in the long run. The behavioural view is that for all practical purposes, all behaviours, both good and bad, are learned and maintained through their consequences. The painful, but inevitable, concomitant of this is that most of the naughty and troublesome acts which children engage in and which are such an embarrassment to teachers and parents have been taught and are being maintained by them through the contingencies which they themselves have provided and continue to provide.

If we go back to the example in Chapter 1 of the little girl on the train, Sharon, who has learned to shout and go on shouting until she gets her parents' attention, we have a clear case of this principle in action. An extension of the principle leads us to the remedy. If behaviour is learned, then it can be unlearned and a new form of behaviour substituted. This behaviour change can be achieved by changing the consequences. It sounds simple and in principle it is so, but in order to change the consequences we have first to change our own behaviour because it is often we who are providing these consequences.

Extinction

The simplest way of decreasing the rate of incidence of a behaviour which is being maintained by attention is to ignore it. If the principle that consequences maintain behaviours is true, then it follows that to withdraw the consequences will cause the behaviour to cease. This process is called *extinction* and it has been shown empirically to be very effective. Unfortunately, there are two drawbacks. First, it may take a long time, and secondly, before it becomes extinguished the frequency of the behaviour may reach very high levels. We have probably all had some experience of the spoiled child in a public place like a park or a supermarket, where he demonstrates his control over his mother through tantrum behaviour. He decides that he wants something, maybe sweets or ice-cream, which his mother does not want him to have. Accordingly, he throws a tantrum – crying, yelling, kicking and throwing himself about. The real 'tantrum experts' have to use only the threat of this kind of behaviour to get what they want. The prototype was Violet Elizabeth Bott in the 'William' books by Richmal Crompton. She would lisp her threat to 'thcweam and thcweam and thcweam 'til I'm thick' so that William was forced to allow her a part in one of his nefarious schemes. Children like these have learned that mother will eventually respond but that sometimes she will hold out for quite a long while. They always get what they want in the end and this inconsistent schedule of rewarding teaches them to be very persistent. If the mother decides that from now on the child is never going to get his way by screaming, and so on, she will have to endure a number of really long, all-out sessions of protest before he learns that *no* amount of tantrum behaviour is going to pay off. This is going to be very hard for the mother.

Before leaving this point it is important to emphasise that attempts at extinction by ignoring will only work if the behaviour really is being maintained by adult attention. Many irritating classroom behaviours are maintained by peer attention and hence no amount of ignoring by the teacher will cause such behaviours to extinguish. It makes sense to attempt to harness the power of the peer group and to use it in your interventions. So-called *group contingency* methods lead to a pay-off for the whole group, contingent upon desired behaviour by the group or an individual within it. A clown is no longer amusing if his antics prevent the whole group from gaining a promised reward.

Punishment

Another way to bring about a decrease in this sort of behaviour is to use an aversive consequence, that is, something the child does not like – a punishment, in fact. If the mother in the supermarket were to administer a sharp slap and march the child straight home as soon as he began his antics, the behaviour might reduce much more rapidly than if she just ignored him. Perhaps in this case, to save her the embarrassment and the inconvenience of everyone concerned, such action could be justified. Being sharp and unexpected it might prove to be very effective, but generally when using the behavioural approach we try to avoid the use of punishment for the reasons already given.

Incompatible Behaviours

If we are not going to use punishment to choke off a behaviour, how then can we reduce its rate of occurrence? The answer is to increase the rate of another behaviour which is *incompatible* with the one we are trying to control. If noisy chattering is the problem, we will do better to encourage quietness. If a child is too often out of his seat, then we can try reinforcing in-seat behaviour. He cannot be seated and wandering about at the same time. These two behaviours are incompatible with each other. If untidiness or lateness is the problem, we could work on increasing tidiness and promptness as behaviours to be encouraged. Once we have redefined the problem in this positive way we can go back to the techniques for increasing behaviour rates which have already been discussed. On the whole, the behavioural approach concentrates on ways of increasing acceptable behaviours and is optimistic and accepting rather than punishing and forbidding.

It may be that our problem is a child who is observed to be out of his seat, talking to and distracting his neighbours twenty or more times in a lesson. Some aspects of the situation are reinforcing him positively when he does this. Ideally we should like to know what these are, so that we can change them, but practically it may be impossible. What we could do is to devise some plan which will give him a bigger 'pay-off' to stay put and get on with his own work. We may agree with him a target of, say, ten 'out of seats' only per lesson to begin with, to be followed by some chosen reward. After a day or two, this criterion having been met, we would change the conditions so that he would be allowed first eight, then six, then four 'out of seats' until he was getting out of his seat no more than the other children, say, once or twice per lesson. If a great deal of social reinforcement has been used throughout the programme, it should now be possible to phase out the intervention. This may be done by gradually changing the time scale and/or contingencies for rewarding until social reinforcement alone is maintaining the in-seat behaviour.

Time-Out

We have suggested that punishment is considered inappropriate by those who advocate the behavioural approach and have given reasons for this, but there are two forms of punishment that are more acceptable. The first of these is *time-out*, a contraction of 'time out from positive reinforcement'. Time-out involves placing a child for a short period, of perhaps two to five minutes, in an environment which is completely without stimulation. After this period is up, he is returned to the classroom environment where, once again, he can earn positive reinforcement for behaving well. The removal of the child to the time-out area must be scheduled to follow certain well-defined behaviours and must be done expeditiously, dispassionately and without argument. When he returns there is to be no recrimination or other comment. He has 'served his time' and is allowed immediately to earn the full benefits of his appropriate behaviour.

Clearly, a good time-out area is not easy to arrange in school and the method is probably going to be most effective with smaller children. However, it has been used effectively with children up to their early 'teens. It bears some resemblance to the practice, common in schools, of putting children in the corner or outside the room or even of sending them to the headteacher. There the resemblance ends, however. A child outside the door has a great opportunity for engaging in conversation with passers-by. Even being placed in the corner allows a child to show off to his friends. Both of these outcomes are potentially highly reinforcing. Sometimes children are more of a nuisance to the teacher outside than they were in the class. Sending to the head can also be counter-productive. The comings and goings in the secretary's room may be infinitely more interesting than what is going on in the classroom. It is not unknown for competitions to develop within a class to see who can be sent out most often!

Response Cost

The second of these more acceptable forms of punishment, *response cost*, can be applied when a child is receiving marks or other tokens for behaviour which satisfies some criterion. For example, he may be receiving a star every time he completes a ten-minute period without leaving his seat. Response cost would then be applied by taking away a star every time he calls out to the teacher without first raising his hand to get permission to speak, a behaviour controlled in an earlier programme. An essential for using this technique is to ensure that a sufficiently high rate of earning is established before response cost is applied. If response cost is allowed to bring about a negative balance the whole programme can be jeopardised since children will rapidly become discouraged.

INTERVENTIONS: SOME OTHER THINGS TO KEEP IN MIND

One aspect of the behavioural approach to classroom management which differentiates it from others is the need to 'think small', which has already been exemplified in many of the illustrations given so far. Very often parents and teachers are reasonably successful in identifying children's problems but in their search for a remedy they aim at a perfect solution immediately. A parent will say, 'If you stop sniffing (meaning that I never want to hear another sniff) I will allow you to stay up and watch your favourite TV programme'. Or a teacher will say, 'Those who get full marks will have a house point'. Targets such as these are quite useless to a child who is sniffing five times a minute or who never completes more than three sums out of ten set. At the beginning of a programme changes are bound to be small. The rate of change will accelerate later, but to begin with, small improvements must be made readily apparent and rewarded appropriately.

One of the clearest examples of this is to be seen in the shaping process where, at first, the response rewarded may bear little relation to the final target behaviour. To be successful a programme must set targets from the outset which are attainable by the subject with a reasonable amount of effort. A child who is calling out to the teacher fifteen times in a lesson cannot reduce this rate to nil at once but, with encouragement, will perhaps be able to manage twelve to start with.

Comment has often been made drawing attention to the fact that the effects of successful interventions seem to 'snowball'. In fact, the effect of reinforcement or the lack of it does seem to carry elements of self-perpetuation. If a child makes attempts to communicate or read or to make any response at all, in fact, and these efforts never receive any positive reinforcement, whether intrinsic or extrinsic, the general effect is bound to be inhibiting. All teachers have met children whose attempts to learn to read have been so lacking in reward of any kind that they have just given up trying. They will go to almost any lengths not to have to try again because they fear failure. Once a child begins to receive positive reinforcement for responding in ways that are acceptable to those around him, success breeds upon success and the process is carried forward by its natural momentum.

Numerous studies of children labelled 'impossible to cope with' tell the same story. Practically everything that these children do seems to engender a negative response from those near to them. These responses, however unlikely it may appear, are, in fact, maintaining the unwanted behaviours. Once a breakthrough is made, in however small an area, the people around the child begin to find opportunities for reinforcing him positively and this, in itself, changes their image of the child. They begin to find something to approve of and to say that there must be some good in him. Once again there is a snowball effect which may, of course, be very slow to develop at first. In some cases of failure to learn appropriately it may be necessary to *engineer* positive reinforcement in the early stages or to arrange for it to occur in abundance for very small changes in behaviour. Sometimes, when a lack of progress is limited to one area, say, reading, it may be better to leave this completely alone for a while and to concentrate on raising self-confidence in another sphere of activity before returning to it, using, as far as possible, a new method of approach.

On the other hand, as has been suggested earlier, success breeds confidence and further success. Once we become accustomed to the approval and praise of others, and most of our efforts at learning and doing are positively reinforced, then we can stand occasional failure. Our confidence is not broken as we begin to depend more and more upon the intrinsic reinforcement provided by accomplishment, as described in Chapter 4.

In setting out the strategies for bringing about behaviour change we have had to deal with them in a certain order. The more difficult and troublesome methods were sometimes described first. This, however, was not meant to suggest that these are the ones that should be tried first – quite the reverse. The heavier the armament you choose to solve your problem, the more trouble it is likely to be and the more disruptive of your normal class routine. By and large we want to choose the most appropriate and least upsetting mode of change. We do not want to use a sledge-hammer to crack a peanut. It has been shown that in certain cases all that is necessary is to spell out for the child, in unequivocal terms, what is expected of him in certain situations. This is often a sufficient change in the setting to bring about a desirable change in the behaviour.

The diagnostic flow-chart at the end of this chapter (Figure 5.1) attempts to set out the hierarchy of stratagems available. Note that in every case we consider antecedents first. These are normally the easiest and lightest interventions to introduce. If they do not work then we consider consequence management strategies, starting with the least intrusive. In ordinary classroom situations simple rules and social rewarding are going to be your strongest suit and will prove to be effective for most interventions whether with an individual or the whole class. If we try a strategy which is too light-weight and so proves to be inadequate we are soon made aware of this and can change it for one that is more effective. Other approaches make little attempt to monitor outcomes in this way and rely upon a casual consensus to conclude whether or not the child's problem has been 'cured'. The behavioural approach, with its emphasis on observing and recording and the constant monitoring of effects, enables us to match our strategy exactly to the presenting problem and to observe its effectiveness

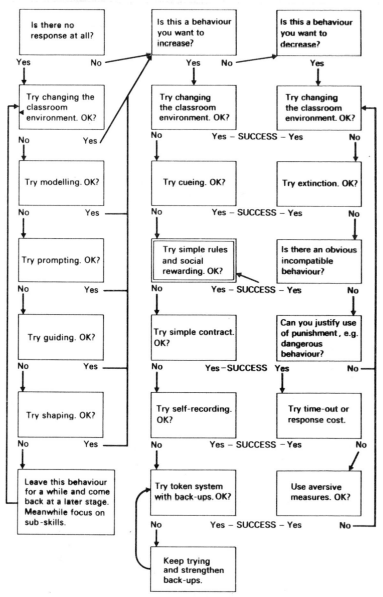

Figure 5.1 *Diagnostic flow-chart for solving behavioural problems in the classroom.* (See note opposite.)

EXERCISES

1.   In your school children are expected to line up in the playground at the end of break periods (separate lines for boys and girls) and you are required to supervise their progress along the corridor and back into the classroom. Your class numbers thirty-four and so the lines are long. The route includes two corners and a set of fire doors which means that you cannot keep the whole class in view. There is thus a degree of noise and confusion. How could you modify the antecedent conditions so as to make the conduct of this exercise quieter and more orderly?

2.   You have a child in your class who *never* volunteers an answer. How can you begin to encourage such a child to take a fuller part in the life of the classroom? Use the diagnostic flow-chart to help you in this.

3.   You have a child in your class who acts in an aggressive way towards other children. He has been observed to do this eight to ten times during the school day. Use the diagnostic flow-chart at the end of this chapter to suggest how best you might begin to tackle this problem.

RECAPITULATION EXERCISES FOR PART ONE

The two exercises which follow give you the opportunity to try out all that you have learned from Part One of this book.

A.   Here is a narrative which uncovers some aspects of the behaviour of a child with a problem.

Mr Green: John Smith has real problems.
Miss White: Yes, I know. I used to teach him last year.
Mr Green: He does not seem to be able to stay in his seat. He's always wandering around the room, to the pencil-sharpener, the art table, my desk, the cupboard; everywhere except where he's supposed to be.
Miss White: What do you do with him?

Note: Once you have succeeded in changing behaviour you must seek to fade the programme so as to maintain the new behaviour rate on naturally occurring positive reinforcement.

Mr Green: I'm constantly having to tell him to sit down, get back to his seat and so on.

Miss White: He was referred to the psychological services last year and they said he was suffering from hyperactivity and would have trouble paying attention in class. He was recommended for Special Education but they could not find a place for him. The social services were also asked for a report and found that the home situation was not too good. They suggested that there was a lack of 'inner control'.

(*a*) Identify the explanatory fictions.
(*b*) Account for the fact that punishing (telling off for being out of seat) does not seem to work.
(*c*) Pinpoint some behaviours that the teacher might observe.
(*d*) Suggest a behavioural approach to John Smith's problems.

B. Choose from the alternatives the completion phrase which is most in line with the behavioural approach.

1. *Teaching is*:

(*a*) a process which involves drawing out what is already within
(*b*) concerned with developing a person's thinking processes
(*c*) concerned with changing behaviour
(*d*) what happens in classrooms.

2. *Learning results from*:

(*a*) practice: the more you practise, the more you learn
(*b*) repeated exposure to a stimulus which forms new stimulus–response bonds
(*c*) high motivation, which makes you want to learn
(*d*) the consequences of our actions.

3. *The biggest influence on future behaviour is*:

(*a*) a person's attitude
(*b*) the consequences of earlier behaviour
(*c*) the concepts that a person forms
(*d*) the feelings a person has.

4. *Our chief concern should always be*:

(*a*)   with the long-term well-being of the person concerned
(*b*)   with the feelings of the parents
(*c*)   that all bad behaviour is ignored
(*d*)   that only positive measures are used.

5. *It may be useful to ignore inappropriate behaviour*:

(*a*)   every time it happens
(*b*)   whenever it is no danger to anyone else
(*c*)   when attention from you has been reinforcing the problem behaviour
(*d*)   when you want the behaviour to occur less frequently.

6. *If you are faced with a problem in which children spend a lot of time out of their seats you should*:

(*a*)   give them plenty of equipment and apparatus so that their activity can be useful
(*b*)   tell them off when they get out of their places
(*c*)   provide more interesting things for them to do when they are seated
(*d*)   devise a plan which will reinforce them positively for being in their seats.

7. *If Mary behaves politely enough in school but is cheeky and rude to her mother at home this is because*:

(*a*)   she is stubborn and thoughtless at home
(*b*)   she has not really learned how to behave
(*c*)   she is reinforced when she is polite at school
(*d*)   she wants to please her teacher more than her mother.

8. *We call children slow learners because*:

(*a*)   they find it difficult to learn new skills
(*b*)   they get low scores on IQ tests
(*c*)   they cannot understand what teachers are telling them
(*d*)   they may know the answers but they cannot tell you.

9. *John spends a lot of his time gazing out of the window because*:

(*a*)   he is bored with school work
(*b*)   school work does not challenge him sufficiently
(*c*)   the work that he does produce is not reinforced
(*d*)   the work that the teacher is providing is not relevant to his immediate needs – he does not see it as useful.

10. *Charles never speaks in class but is always chattering to his friends in the playground. This is because*:

(*a*)   he uses a language code which is only appropriate in the playground
(*b*)   he is a stupid child who cannot respond to the teacher's questions
(*c*)   he likes playing but does not like learning
(*d*)   he finds the attention of his peers in the playground reinforcing.

11. *The children in class 2B work better for Miss Green than for Mr Cardew. This is because*:

(*a*)   Miss Green has a more kindly manner
(*b*)   Mr Cardew treats the girls more favourably than the boys
(*c*)   Miss Green is better at giving appropriate encouragement to the children
(*d*)   Mr Cardew does not get on as well with the children.

12. *If you are successfully ignoring a particular 'attention-seeking' behaviour you will expect*:

(*a*)   the behaviour to extinguish
(*b*)   the behaviour to increase
(*c*)   the behaviour to increase at first and then to extinguish
(*d*)   the behaviour to be replaced by another to gain your attention.

13. *You are helping a rather slow child to master a complex manipulative skill (for example, doing up a series of buttons). You should*:

(*a*)   stop giving help, wait for him to succeed and then reward him

(*b*)   wait until he fails and then help him
(*c*)   help him almost to the end, leave him to finish (like pushing the last and easiest button through the hole) and then reward him
(*d*)   help with the hardest bits leaving him to do the easier ones.

14   *Which of those statements best pinpoints a behaviour*.

(*a*)   John stood on his chair for six seconds
(*b*)   Mary showed her anger for one whole minute
(*c*)   Charlie is overactive
(*d*)   Susan is always trying to attract attention to herself.

15.   *Positive reinforcers are*:

(*a*)   things that can be eaten or drunk
(*b*)   things that make an action more likely to happen again
(*c*)   things that teachers and parents use to reward children
(*d*)   special things that are used to modify behaviour.

16.   *If a young child displays a great deal of tantrum behaviour we can say that*:

(*a*)   he enjoys being the centre of attention
(*b*)   he must have been born with that sort of stubborn temperament
(*c*)   he must have suffered a great deal of frustration as a baby
(*d*)   he has been taught to behave that way by his parents.

17.   *Vicarious learning (modelling) is where*:

(*a*)   children learn something by watching films or television
(*b*)   children are taught by visiting clergy
(*c*)   children learn by watching the behaviour of others and what happens to them
(*d*)   children learn by their own, first-hand experience.

18.   *Sometimes behaviour change can be brought about by changing the antecedent conditions (settings). This means*:

(*a*)   changing some element(s) in the environmental situation for the child

(*b*) changing the consequences of the child's behaviour
(*c*) making sure that the child is punished where he has previously been rewarded
(*d*) changing the contingencies in a contract.

19. *Sometimes behaviour which a teacher is trying to change is being maintained by the child's peers. In this case we have to*:

(*a*) contrive a punishing contingency for peers when they reinforce the child's behaviour
(*b*) use counter-control
(*c*) use a 'reinforcement of any other behaviour' schedule
(*d*) make the reinforcing event apply to the whole group.

20. *Punishment should be avoided in behavioural interventions because*:

(*a*) it does not work
(*b*) it works only in certain circumstances
(*c*) it is not ethical for one person to control the behaviour of another
(*d*) it has a number of unwanted side-effects.

Part Two

Analysing Classroom Behaviour and Demonstration Studies

Chapter 6

Analysing Classroom Behaviour: Making Sense of your Data

In Part One of this book we covered, in some detail, the theoretical model and methodology of the behavioural approach and its applications to teaching. Part Two consists primarily of a series of classroom demonstration studies designed and carried out by teachers in their own classrooms. Most of these studies present data collected and recorded in ways already described in Chapter 3. But these data really come to life when we draw graphs of them and the practical effects of the interventions become clearly visible. This is shown in several of the classroom intervention studies which employ graphs. In this chapter we will introduce simple graphing techniques. Far from being a chore, graphing can be one of the most exciting aspects of the approach. Nothing is more reinforcing for teachers who adopt this behavioural approach than to see their graph daily demonstrate the effectiveness of their interventions.

GRAPHING THE BASELINE PHASE

In Chapter 3 we discussed in some detail ways of observing and recording behaviour in the classroom. Prior to any intervention it is important to collect data in order to gain a clear picture of the current frequency of the behaviour and the circumstances in which it occurs. This is what we call *baseline* data. Once you have a record covering several days of observations it becomes necessary to arrange and summarise your data in order to see if any pattern is

Table 6.1 Completed Schedule for Peter's 'Calling Out' Behaviour

Session	a.m.								Total	p.m.								Total
	1	2	3	4	5	6	7	8		1	2	3	4	5	6	7	8	
Monday	3	4	7	5	5	6	5		35	9	10	8	11	12				50
Tuesday	5	4	3	6	7	5			30	8	9	7	6	10				40
Wednesday	6	8	7	7					28	7	9	9	6	11	12			54
Thursday	4	5	6	8	7	6	6		42	7	6	9	8	10				40
Friday	5	6	5	4	7	5	3		35	7	9	9	12	11	12			60

beginning to emerge. The best device for this purpose is a graph. Do not be put off by this idea as only the simplest sort of graph is necessary. There are several points to bear in mind, however. If you have been observing events for a different number of time-periods each day it will be no good drawing graphs of your results as they stand, since they will not be comparable.

Let us take an example, based on a schedule like the one shown in Table 3.1 in Chapter 3. You recall that this schedule provided records of Peter's 'calling out' behaviour as shown in Table 6.1. Each number in Table 6.1 is the result of five minutes of observation. For example, the first observation of the week (under 1 for Monday) shows that Peter was heard to speak three times, in the second four times, and so on. You can see, however, that it would be pointless to draw a graph of the totals as they stand since the number of observation sessions varies. Before we can proceed to draw a graph we have to calculate the average or mean score separately for each morning and afternoon. On Monday morning

Table 6.2   *Average Numbers of Peter's 'Calling Out' Behaviours per half day*

		No. of events	No. of sessions	Mean
Monday	a.m.	35	7	5
	p.m.	50	5	10
Tuesday	a.m.	30	6	5
	p.m.	40	5	8
Wednesday	a.m.	28	4	7
	p.m.	54	6	9
Thursday	a.m.	42	7	6
	p.m.	40	5	8
Friday	a.m.	35	7	5
	p.m.	60	6	10

the total number of 'calling out' behaviours observed was 35 and the number of sessions was 7. (Notice that these figures can be read directly from the schedule and this is another good reason for keeping records of your observations in this way. It is rather like keeping a mark- or record-book of your children's work rather than writing things down on the back of your shopping-list or a cigarette packet.) Thus the average number of events for Monday morning would be 35 (total number of events) divided by 7 (number of sessions) which equals 5. We can calculate the means for each morning and afternoon as shown in Table 6.2.

We are now in a position to draw the graph, and one way of doing it would be as in Figure 6.1 where each score is plotted in succession for each half day. The observation periods run along the bottom of the graph whilst the mean number of calling out events is shown on the vertical axis. For each observation period we plot the mean number of calling out events recorded as a point on the graph and join them up.

Looking at this graph we can begin to see the patterns that are emerging. The graph has an appearance of instability. It seems to be going up and down all the time but this enables us to see that the means for the mornings are lower than those for the

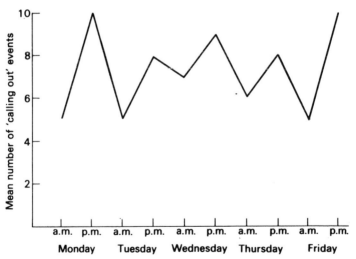

Figure 6.1   *Graph to show the incidence of Peter's 'calling out' behaviour.*

Table 6.3   *Average Number of Peter's 'Calling Out' Behaviours per Day*

	No. of events	No. of sessions	Mean rate
Monday	85	12	7·1
Tuesday	70	11	6·4
Wednesday	82	10	8·2
Thursday	82	12	6·8
Friday	95	13	7·3

afternoons, that is, Peter appears to be calling out more in the afternoons than in the mornings. We could get rid of these fluctuations by using the data to produce a graph showing the rates for each day, that is, by working out the means for each whole day (as in Table 6.3) and drawing another graph as in Figure 6.2.

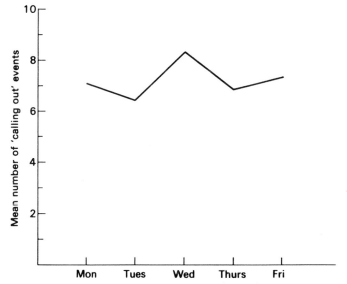

Figure 6.2   *Graph to show the incidence of Peter's 'calling out' behaviour (daily averages).*

A graph like this is much more stable than the one we had before but it obscures some aspects of the data and does not show the important fact that the results for mornings and afternoons differ from one another. To show this we need to go back to our original figures (Table 6.2) and plot them for mornings and afternoons separately, on the same graph, as shown in Figure 6.3. This graph shows us clearly that the behaviours are occurring at different rates from morning to afternoon and it may be possible to find out what is causing this difference. If we can, it could well provide a vital clue to the best sort of intervention.

Either Figure 6.2 or Figure 6.3 could now be taken as representing the usual rate of Peter's 'calling out' behaviour and is, in fact, the baseline. It represents the rate at which Peter has been calling out up to this point and will give us something to compare with when we have decided what intervention procedures to carry out. So long as we are sure that we have identified some action which is an observable and countable feature of the behaviour we are interested in, and the graph for this data is more or less stable, we can proceed to the next step. In very rare instances, when we

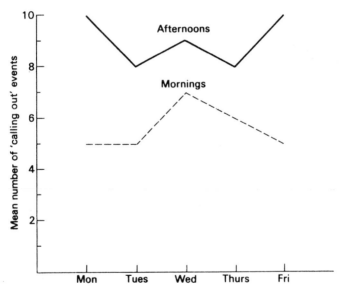

Figure 6.3   *Graph to show the incidence of Peter's 'calling out' behaviour (separate averages for mornings and afternoons).*

are trying to teach absolutely new behaviours, for instance, the baseline level may be nil. Perhaps the child never says 'Thank you' or never puts up his hand to ask a question. Such baseline data would, of course, be absolutely stable. The importance of such stability will be discussed shortly.

The next question we might ask is, 'How long does the baseline period need to be?' With the degree of stability that we can see on Figures 6.2 and 6.3 we might be content. Certainly another week, at most, would be quite sufficient. Something between seven and ten days of stable data is usually regarded as a good base, but there are times when the situation is desperate and we may be prepared to proceed with less than this amount of baseline data. Sometimes the careful observation of what is believed to be a problem behaviour makes the observer aware that, in fact, the rate of occurrence of this behaviour is at quite a low level and that it is some other, and quite unexpected, behaviour that is causing the trouble. This may very well be the case with some quiet children, since a lot of their behaviour goes unnoticed in the ordinary classroom situation until someone begins to look very carefully. A child in a junior school who produced a very small output of work was suspected by the teacher (one of our students) to be very withdrawn and to have almost no contact with the other children in the class. Careful observation of this child's behaviour by the headteacher of the school, who was asked by the teacher to help with the task of observing, revealed that this girl spent a considerable amount of her time out of her seat and chatting with the other children. She did this very quietly so that the class teacher had not really taken account of it, but this was the real reason that the child did so little work.

Sometimes, directly a behaviour is observed it begins to change. This could be the reason for the unstable baseline. Sometimes it seems to disappear altogether. This is what has been termed the 'disappearing problem', which we referred to in Chapter 3, and it doubtless has to do with the fact that as soon as a teacher begins to look at a behaviour which has proved to be troublesome, her very awareness causes her to respond to it (unwittingly) in a different way. We try to collect baseline data surreptitiously and without changing our response to it, but this is very difficult to do. A teacher may decide that a child's 'calling out' behaviour needs to be changed for the benefit of everyone and she begins to observe the behaviour in order to obtain a baseline. In observing, however, she becomes aware that she is constantly nagging this child about his behaviour. This awareness may cause her to reduce her nagging to some extent and may be all that is necessary to change the child's behaviour. The calling out no longer receives its former high rate of attention from the teacher and is extinguished naturally. This control of behaviour by teachers is going on all the time but we are largely unaware of it. Incidentally, children control teachers' behaviours in much the same way.

It is very important for us to maintain our behaviour whilst we are collecting baseline data. If we fail to do so we may not actually get rid of the behaviour we are observing but we may cause a trend to develop. Obviously, if we want to reduce a particular behaviour and our observing causes a downward trend in the baseline data then the effect, when we finally apply our intervention, is going to be much less dramatic than otherwise. (Of course, if our chief concern is the reduction of the behaviour it does not matter much either way, but you would probably prefer to feel that you are in control of the process and to have some idea about what is changing the behaviour.) We do not stop collecting data when we have completed the baseline, however. If we go on collecting and graphing our data we shall be able to see clearly the effects of any intervention strategies that we decide to use. This is why it is important for the task of observation to be as simple and straightforward as possible.

GRAPHING THE INTERVENTION PHASE

After we have collected a sample of observations to obtain a baseline we shall be interested to see the effects of our intervention strategy. We continue to collect data on the behaviour in exactly the same way as we did during the baseline phase and we continue to graph it. If, within a short period of beginning the planned intervention, the graph changes markedly in direction, we can probably attribute this to our efforts provided that we can be reasonably sure that there have been no other gross changes in the total situation. However, if the baseline data have been very unstable, as in Figure 6.4, or already showing an upward trend, as in Figure 6.5, this would be very difficult to determine. In Figure 6.4 the upward trend beyond the intervention point could be the continuation of a very spasmodic baseline. In Figure 6.5 it would be very difficult to sustain a claim to have brought about this continued slight increase in an already established upward trend, through our intervention. (Note that it is a convention *not* to

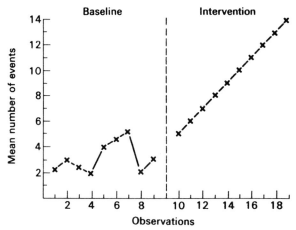

Figure 6.4 *Graph showing an unstable baseline.*

continue the line of the graph across observational phases: in these examples, between observations 9 and 10. This allows changes in behaviour between phases to be readily apparent.)

On the other hand, if the baseline had been completely stable, as in Figure 6.6, we should have much more convincing evidence of having brought about the improvement in behaviour shown by

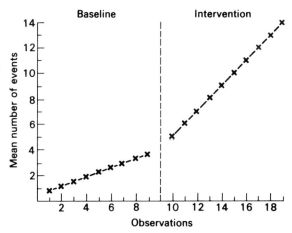

Figure 6.5 *Graph showing a rising baseline.*

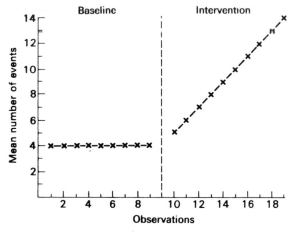

Figure 6.6   *Graph showing a stable baseline.*

the upward movement of the graph. In Figure 6.7 comparison of the baseline with the graph after intervention shows a clear reversal in trend to show that our actions are very probably having some effect upon the child's behaviour. (Note that all these examples are exaggerated to underline the points we are making about baseline levels of behaviour.)

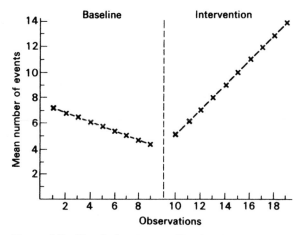

Figure 6.7   *Graph showing a falling baseline.*

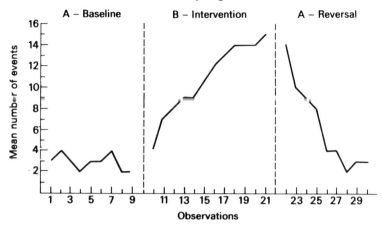

Figure 6.8 *Graph to show the ABA or reversal design.*

In the hard-core scientific research from which the theory behind the behavioural approach has been derived, a great deal of effort has been expended to demonstrate convincing control over behaviour. Some of this has been carried over into applied behavioural research with children and others. One of the most straightforward of the methods used is known as the ABA or reversal design. Careful collection of observational data is used to demonstrate that the intervention carried out is having an effect upon the child's behaviour and, once this is established, the process is reversed. That is, the intervention is withdrawn and the original situation restored. Then if the child's behaviour shows a return to the baseline level, control of the intervention strategy has been demonstrated beyond reasonable doubt (see Figure 6.8). Often such a reversal is difficult to achieve and in the school or family context is regarded by many as counter-productive or even un-ethical. For the teacher this is not a problem since you are in the business of changing behaviour, not of convincing others that you have been able to do so.

ESTIMATING THE RELIABILITY OF YOUR OBSERVATIONS

It is important, if at all possible, to try to check on your objectivity as an observer. One way of doing this is to have someone else observe at the same time using exactly the same method and subject(s) and an identical schedule. The results of half an hour or so of such joint observation can then be compared in order to determine the reliability of your observing and recording. If a timing device is used, where some signal cues the observers to count up the number of children on task, the results would have to be compared, signal for signal, against each other.

Suppose you are able to get someone to come into your classroom to act as a second observer and they produce a record like that below for the Monday morning, using the schedule as given in Table 3.1:

Session   1 2 3 4 5 6 7   Total
Monday   3 3 7 5 6 6 5   35 (your helper's results)

Let us assume that your results for the same period were:

Monday   3 4 7 5 5 6 5   35 (your results)

Now you will observe that your totals are the same, but this does not mean that you are in agreement throughout. Whilst you are in agreement for observation intervals 1, 3, 4, 6 and 7 there is a difference of one for each of the intervals 2 and 5. So whilst you agree completely on the figures 3, 7, 5, 6 and 5 for intervals 1, 3, 4, 6 and 7 respectively, you only agree 3 times for interval 2 and 5 times for interval 5. Overall, then, we have 34 agreements and 2 disagreements. To calculate the level of agreement of our observations (known technically as inter-observer agreement) we use the following formula: inter-observer agreement equals the number of agreements multiplied by one hundred, divided by the number of agreements added to the number of disagreements. In this case, the inter-observer agreement was calculated as follows:

$$\frac{34 \times 100}{34 + 2} = \frac{3400}{36} = 94 \cdot 4 \text{ per cent.}$$

Of course, we have no guarantee that the seven 'calling out' incidents that you tallied for session three were exactly the same seven that your second observer tallied, but since it is the rate of responding in which we are chiefly interested, we can have a fair degree of confidence in the objectivity of our method of data collection since your rates for the morning are the same, namely five. If your measure of inter-observer agreement is over 90 per cent then you have reached a very high level of agreement.

Anything above 80 can be regarded as satisfactory, but clearly the higher it is the better.

You do not have to carry out an inter-observer agreement check every time you observe it but it is a good idea to carry out such a check before you begin to collect baseline data. If you cannot get a reasonable level of agreement with a colleague then your definitions or your method of observation are suspect. It is a good idea to have at least one more check on inter-observer agreement later in your work, if at all possible, because, as in other spheres, 'familiarity breeds contempt'. Your observing may become less and less accurate without your knowing it.

Having said all this about the desirability of collecting estimates of inter-observer agreement it is important to stress that it is not essential for the classroom teacher – unless you want to publish your results! Your main concern should be to keep accurate records and to graph them in order to determine the effectiveness of your interventions. Our main purpose in this chapter has been to suggest ways in which this may be done systematically and without distracting you too much from your chief job which is, of course, teaching.

EXERCISES

1.   A teacher has a problem with a boy who always seems to be out of his seat. She decides to watch him for fifteen minutes in the morning and fifteen minutes in the afternoon and enters her findings in a table, as below. Comment upon her method and draw a graph of the results.

Response definition – whenever Harry is not sitting down.

Time for counting   – 10.00 to 10.15 every morning and 2.00 to 2.15 every afternoon to be scored by tallying.

Results	a.m.	p.m.
Monday	8	4
Tuesday	9	3
Wednesday	10	6
Thursday	12	3
Friday	8	4

2.   Suppose you have been collecting data about a boy's 'out of seat' behaviour. You have a clear definition of this behaviour and persuade a colleague to spend fifteen minutes in your classroom observing the child's behaviour with you. You both observe him every time the sweep hand of the classroom clock points at the twelve, putting a cross for out of seat. The results are tabulated below. Calculate the measure of agreement and comment on its adequacy. We will concern ourselves only with occurrences of 'out of seat' behaviour, not non-occurrences. Inclusion of non-occurrence agreements would tend to inflate the size of the reliability measure.

2

	1	2	3	4	5	6	7	8	9	10	11	12	13	14	15
Your observations		×	×		×		×		×		×	×		×	
Colleague's observations		×	×		×		×				×	×		×	

3.   In this case you are concerned to record on-task behaviour. You look at a certain table on hearing a signal and write down the number of children who are on-task at that instant, according to your definition. You teach the procedure to a student teacher who is working with you and she observes with you for a period. The results are as follows. Calculate the measure of agreement. Would you be satisfied with this?

3

Observation	1	2	3	4	5	6	7	8	9	10	11	12	13	14	15
Your results	5	4	4	3	5	5	2	4	5	4	3	5	5	4	5
Student's results	5	4	5	4	5	5	3	5	4	4	3	5	4	5	5

4.   Jan is concerned about the small amount of work produced by her class of thirty children. Casual observation suggests that they spend a lot of time chatting and moving about unnecessarily and, consequently, spend little time on their work-cards. She decides to observe on-task behaviour which she pinpoints to her satisfaction and collects data on this for half an hour every morning for ten days using an audible signal and an observation schedule.

Following this baseline phase she implements a 'rules, ignore and praise' procedure and continues to collect data for a further ten days. For the next five days she abandons the 'rules, ignore and praise' procedure and then reinstates it, keeping up her recording of data throughout.

The table below details Jan's data collected over seven weeks. The daily on-task behaviour of the class is expressed as a percentage. Draw a graph of Jan's data, calculate the mean for each phase and comment upon the effectiveness of her intervention.

4

Days	1	2	3	4	5	6	7	8	9	*10*	*11*	*12*	*13*	*14*	*15*	*16*	*17*
% on-task	60	50	45	65	70	50	50	55	50	55	65	75	85	90	90	85	85

Days	*18*	*19*	*20*	*21*	*22*	*23*	*24*	*25*	*26*	*27*	*28*	*29*	*30*	*31*	*32*	*33*	*34*
% on-task	90	85	90	70	60	65	55	60	70	85	90	95	90	89	92	85	87

Chapter 7

Interventions with Individual Children

In the final two chapters of this book we report a series of demonstration studies carried out by teachers in their own classrooms. The first six studies, which are presented in this chapter, report interventions carried out with individual children. The following chapter (8) reports studies carried out with groups, usually whole classes. In each chapter we begin by describing work with younger children and then move up through the age range.

Most of these studies were implemented without any additional help, apart from advice and guidance by the authors. The various studies exemplify the behavioural approach to teaching over a wide range of ages and teaching contexts. We hope that these studies will be helpful in two ways: first, to convey the 'feel' of the behavioural approach in practice, how it works in the real world; and secondly, as models for possible interventions which you could adapt for your own specific purposes.

Each classroom demonstration study is presented within the same format. *Setting* provides the details of the problem and the context in which it occurs. *Method* outlines how the behaviour was pinpointed and recorded and gives details of the intervention strategy employed. *Results* reports the outcome of the intervention including details of any data collected, where appropriate. Finally, *Comments* includes discussion of the outcome of the intervention by the authors and/or the teacher involved and suggestions for improvement.

It should be noted that not all of the studies report 'hard' data. Since the teachers involved were carrying out their regular duties at the same time, it was not always possible to achieve the elegance and sophistication of traditional laboratory-based research in terms of design or data collection. 'Research' of this nature, in the real world, carried out by teachers who are, perhaps rightly, more interested in immediate outcomes than establishing scientific truths, is often like this. There is no shortage of reports of carefully designed and controlled studies which meet traditional scientific criteria, and you will find reference to these in our suggestions for further reading at the end of this book. Our purpose here is to report studies carried out by ordinary teachers in everyday situations with the aim of inspiring you to use the behavioural approach in original and creative ways.

CLASSROOM DEMONSTRATION STUDY 1

ENCOURAGING A BASIC SKILL AT THE INFANT LEVEL

Setting

A 6-year-old girl in the second year of an infant school was not copying her first name correctly. The teacher had tried persuasion and various kinds of encouragement but nothing seemed to be effective. The teacher suspected that the child could perform the task but that, for some reason, she was reluctant to do so. The teacher had lately become so frustrated by the lack of progress and apparent lack of effort from the child that she had been resorting to 'punishment' (finger-tapping) for every mistake, as a last resort. The result of this was complete disharmony and a sense of confrontation between the child and the teacher.

Method

The teacher decided to try the behavioural approach and to concentrate on the positive aspects of the situation. She decided to abandon punishment, to do her utmost not to react emotionally (as she had been doing) and to praise the child for every letter that she formed correctly.

Results

On the next occasion when the child was required to copy her name the teacher supplied the model and then stood nearby while the child made her attempt. Every time the child successfully completed a letter the teacher responded with warm praise. The child completed her name without error for the first time and has continued to do so ever since. Two weeks later she was writing her first and second names correctly from memory.

Comments

Here we have a clear case of unproductive behaviour (what many teachers and parents would call stubborn behaviour) being maintained by the teacher. When the teacher was trying to be encouraging she was probably using a reinforcer that the child did not find positive. Alternatively, she was using it incorrectly, that is, not contingently, or perhaps not immediately or abundantly enough. Her frustration with the failure of these methods became greater and greater so she began to use what she thought to be punishing consequences. In fact, these may have been serving to *maintain* the behaviour. When these consequences were effectively changed and positive reinforcement was applied contingently, immediately and abundantly, its effect was felt at once and behaviour change took place. Note that the skill was, in effect, already present; what was lacking was the will to perform it. In other words, it was not a matter of teaching a task but of providing an incentive.

CLASSROOM DEMONSTRATION STUDY 2

IMPROVING THE CLASSROOM BEHAVIOUR OF A 7-YEAR-OLD BOY IN AN EDUCATIONAL ASSESSMENT UNIT

Setting

This study was concerned with an attempt to improve the general classroom behaviour of a 7-year-old boy, Ted, who had been placed in an educational assessment unit in a Birmingham primary school. At the time of the commencement of this study he had been attending the unit for one week as a member of a class of ten children aged from 6 to 11, staffed by a teacher and a classroom assistant. In an educational psychologist's report on Ted the following terms had been used: overactive, defiant, non-conforming, impulsive and lacks control, experiencing learning difficulties and very poor attention skills.

Classroom observation showed him to display a high level of attention-seeking behaviour. His disruptive acts appeared to have been reinforced by the attention these had aroused in both parents and previous teachers. He had apparently been given a lot of attention for his 'odd' behaviour: for example, his parents had often been known to comment on his antics, with some amusement, within the child's hearing. This is not uncommon, of course, with such cases. The amount of work he produced was minimal which is not surprising in view of the time he spent off-task (that is, out of his seat, staring at the ceiling or at other children). The reward system of praise, stars and sweets, already in operation in the class, appeared to be having no effect on Ted.

Method

It was originally decided to attempt to reduce Ted's 'out of seat' behaviour. The proposed plan was to observe Ted for half an hour daily for one week to establish a baseline and then to implement a strategy whereby 'out of seat' behaviour would be ignored and on-task behaviour would be reinforced by praise and attention. However, before a full week of observations could be completed the 'out of seat' behaviour had extinguished. It was decided, therefore, to attempt to increase on-task behaviour using the Premack principle, that is, to make an activity that the child was fond of doing dependent upon a satisfactory level of on-task behaviour.

Two ten-minute observations were taken every morning whilst the children were engaged in academic work. During these periods the observer (classroom teacher or her assistant) sampled Ted's behaviour by observing him covertly for a period of five seconds at the end of each thirty seconds. By this means twenty entries relating to Ted's on-task behaviour were available for each ten-minute observation session. Carefully defined, agreed definitions were used and clear criteria set up. For some periods both the teacher and her assistant were able to observe together.

The rules of the intervention were explained to Ted in these terms: if he finished his piece of assigned work quickly, neatly and without too many mistakes he would be allowed to play with the plasticene (a very popular activity with him) for five minutes. This five-minute play period was controlled by means of a kitchen timer. A reversal design was used. Once the baseline (three days) and intervention data (six days) were complete, the intervention was dropped (for three days) and then resumed (for four days),

Results

Inter-observer agreement over the five sessions when joint observation was possible was very high (over 97 per cent). This suggests that the behaviour had been well defined and was being accurately recorded. The graph in Figure 7.1 shows the variation in the levels of on-task behaviour from phase to phase of the intervention. During the first, baseline phase on-task behaviour averaged 20·5 per cent, with the baseline graph falling. When the intervention strategy was introduced, on-task behaviour was greatly increased to a mean level of 70·5 per cent. For the next three days (return to baseline, that is, no contingent reward) it fell rapidly, almost to pre-intervention levels (mean 37·5 per cent), but when the strategy was restored, on-task behaviour returned to its previous high rate averaging 88 per cent. These data clearly demonstrate control of such behaviour by this intervention strategy.

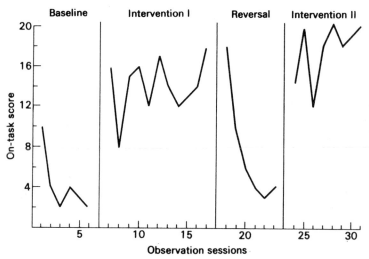

Figure 7.1   *Scores for Ted's observed on-task behaviour.*

Comments

Here we have a good example of the use of the Premack principle and one in which the nature and duration of the reinforcing activity were carefully controlled and defined from the start. Since two adults were working together it was possible to obtain some useful information about the reliability of the data collection and this, to some extent, offset the rather brief periods involved in the successive stages of the intervention. The definition of the work demands could have been tighter but, nevertheless, this proved to be a very simple yet effective strategy.

CLASSROOM DEMONSTRATION STUDY 3

CONTROLLING 'OUT OF SEAT' BEHAVIOUR OF TWO CHILDREN IN A JUNIOR CLASS

Setting

This was a class of 7- and 8-year-olds in a junior school in the West Midlands. The target children were a boy and a girl who were not able to remain in their seats during group work. As a result the boy was interfering with other children whilst the girl rarely produced the work she was capable of doing. They both found all sorts of reasons, like the need to sharpen a pencil, for not getting on with the task in hand.

Method

The teacher observed both children carefully for one day without either becoming aware, and counted the number of times each was out of his/her seat. The scores were 16 for Mark and 14 for Rebecca. The next day she had a talk with both of them and asked them if they knew why she sometimes became angry with them. They suggested many reasons such as 'Forgetting my pencil', 'Losing my reading-book' and 'Chewing my ruler' but did not refer to being out of their places. The teacher, therefore, showed them the results of her observations and they were both impressed by the large numbers. She told them that she would be watching them again and that if the number of 'out of seat' scores dropped they would receive a team point and that this would continue day by day. She showed them charts that she had prepared for each of them on which she would plot the results. She placed these charts at the front of the class for all to see. They both seemed to be excited by the idea.

Results

The teacher watched the children carefully for the next few days and noted that they appeared to help each other by reminding the other of the reward and telling each other to sit down when necessary. Every day the teacher showed Mark and Rebecca their charts and reinforced the team point that they invariably received with praise and encouragement. During the course of the day she would make comments such as 'Careful Mark, I've already noticed five times' or 'I'm still watching, Rebecca'. The children seemed to like the idea behind this programme and pestered the teacher every morning from the moment they walked into the room to see their charts (Table 7.1).

The charts show clearly that the number of times out of seat for each child soon declined until after a day or two both were out of their seats no more than would seem reasonable for most of the other children. These scores became very stable by the third week.

Comments

This intervention was very easy to set up, cost nothing and was very effective. The teacher expressed satisfaction with the success of the programme but said that she felt guilty and sorry for the other children who every day remain in their seats and do not gain team points. Behaviourally, we would justify this by suggesting, on the one hand, that if children are staying in their seats and getting on with their work then that behaviour is being maintained for

Table 7.1 *Number of Occasions when Children Were out of their Seats*

| Mark | | | | | Rebecca | | | | |
Mon	Tues	Wed	Thurs	Fri	Mon	Tues	Wed	Thurs	Fri
		16	10	2			14	9	6
0	0	2	3	2	4	0	2	2	2
1	1	1	1	2	1	1	0	1	1
2	2	2	3	2	2	2	2	2	4

them by consequences which are already being provided by the teacher, the task itself, or by both together. On the other hand, one could suggest that Mark and Rebecca have been taught a more adaptive behaviour by this device. The next task would be to arrange for its maintenance after 'fading' the extrinsic reinforcement of points to the more general social reinforcement that the others also were receiving.

CLASSROOM DEMONSTRATION STUDY 4

CURING A 'PENCIL-CHEWER'

Setting

Jack was an 8-year-old boy in his first year at a middle school situated in an estate of new houses in the Midlands. He entered the school in September bringing with him a record and long history of severe antisocial behaviour which had been dealt with by lengthy periods of isolation. It was decided to work on a minor problem to begin with, namely chewing pencils, almost to the point of eating them.

Method

The headmaster of the school, who undertook the intervention, decided to pinpoint the behaviour as 'chewing the end of the pencil'. He observed the boy for two half-hour periods, one in the morning and one in the afternoon. This was done surreptitiously whilst the head was in the classroom as a matter of routine. The results were as shown in Table 7.2.

Thus an approximate baseline level was obtained.

Jack was given a new pencil first thing in the morning and told that if it was unchewed at the end of the day he would receive 10p.

Table 7.2 *Number of Times Jack Was Seen to be Chewing his Pencil*

Morning	11
Afternoon	6

The headmaster entered the room where Jack was working four or five times during that day (this was according to normal routine) and each time Jack held up his pencil to show that it was unmarked. The headmaster congratulated him each time and gave him warm praise for his achievement so far.

Results

At the end of the day the pencil was quite unmarked and Jack received his reward, as promised. The effects were long lasting. Now, he only occasionally chews his pencil, certainly not noticeably more than other children. The expenditure of 10p and a lot of encouragement worked better than punishment in this case.

Comments

An interesting sidelight on this story is that whilst fulfilling his contract with the headmaster Jack was an absolute pest in class for the whole day – much worse than usual, in fact. The other children felt that it was not really fair that he should be rewarded whilst he was behaving so badly. This underlines the specificity of behaviour and the need to work systematically with the behaviour problems of children who have a long history of unsatisfactory adjustment. It is to be noted that only one well-defined behaviour was dealt with at a time. For a child with a long history of behaviour problems it often appears impossible to find *any* behaviour for which positive reinforcement can be given. Once he begins to receive positive reinforcement for small specific acts he can begin to respond in more adaptive ways and people around begin to see him as other than totally bad. This is a big breakthrough into the vicious circle which is sometimes caused by labelling a child as a bad, hopeless case.

CLASSROOM DEMONSTRATION STUDY 5

CONTROLLING THE TANTRUM BEHAVIOUR OF AN 11-YEAR-OLD CHILD

Setting

David was an 11-year old with a long history of temper tantrums in school (about three every fortnight). During these outbursts of temper he became violent towards others and his language was foul. When he was scolded for this or other sorts of bad behaviour he would often display a sneering sort of truculence. Generally, his scholastic standards were low, but the teacher's main concern was the likely continuation of these outbursts as he became bigger and stronger.

Method

A chart was constructed, as in Table 7.3, in which each day was divided into five sessions. David was shown this chart and told that if he controlled his temper and refrained from truculence for one session, including the lunch-time break, he would have a tick put in the appropriate space. If he succeeded in recording a day full of ticks, he would receive a house point. If, at the end of the week, he had scored five house points he would be entitled to an extra one as a bonus. During the two weeks for which the first phase of this programme ran there was a marked improvement in his behaviour.

The teacher now decided to involve the boy's mother in the second phase. The nature of the intervention was explained to her and she agreed to co-operate, as David's outbursts occurred quite frequently at home also and caused a lot of trouble. The mother reported that David's father regularly lost his temper and gave way to aggression so that a very poor model was provided at home, at times. New targets were set and agreed between David and his mother and the teacher. The same charts were to be used, but to gain a tick David now had to show 'effort' by voluntarily reading to his mother. No house points were to be given for behaviour in

Table 7.3   *David's Token Chart*

	Mon	*Tues*	*Wed*	*Thurs*	*Fri*	
Session 1						before break a.m.
Session 2						after break a.m.
Session 3						lunch-time
Session 4						before break p.m.
Session 5						after break p.m.

school but a report was to go home from the teacher on Fridays. If the report was good a small reward was to be provided by the parents. This had to be something quite small since the family had financial problems, but the size of the reward in a situation like this is unimportant. The mother kept a behaviour chart going for the weekends and one for reading as well. If David was able to control his temper at home and willingly read two pages per day of his reading book his mother sent a favourable report to the teacher, who gave a reward of five house points. After three weeks David had improved in many ways.

After this programme had been running for five weeks the teacher decided that the house point reward was no longer necessary for David to control his behaviour and that praise alone could be used to maintain it. Accordingly, in the third phase the charts were abandoned and replaced by a small notebook entitled 'Effort'. It was agreed that the teacher would write a report in this book on Fridays relating to David's self-control and attitude during the week. If this was satisfactory the mother would reward this outcome at home as before. On Monday mornings the book would be returned to the teacher with a report on behaviour at home and the amount of reading achieved, with a note on the attitude to reading. Under this system both teacher and parent were co-operating to produce a record of progress made.

Results

In the first two-week phase David's behaviour improved dramatically and he earned twenty-three points each week. In the second phase further improvement was apparent. He had been making more effort, he had not lost his temper at all in school and had read to his mother on an average of five out of seven nights. In the third phase, which lasted six weeks, David lost his temper only once although he had been teased and picked upon by other children on several occasions. Over the same six weeks he showed reluctance to read on only two evenings. The teacher reported that reading, written work and attitudes towards others had all improved.

Comments

This project is a good demonstration of the value of parental involvement, brought about here through contracting. It is also a good example of the use of fading extrinsic reinforcement towards social reinforcement, which is more natural, and of extending the time scale. From a behavioural point of view it would perhaps have been better to keep to more objective criteria. For example, 'effort' is very difficult to measure. It might have been better to have defined it in terms of outcome, the amount of work done in a given time, for example. Again, one might ask, what is reluctant reading compared with any other kind? A more objective measure might have been in terms of latency or persistence. In behavioural interventions a little counting is worth a mint of speculation. However, these are minor criticisms of an interesting and successful intervention.

CLASSROOM DEMONSTRATION STUDY 6

USING SELF-RECORDING TO IMPROVE THE BEHAVIOUR OF A 13-YEAR-OLD BOY IN A SECONDARY REMEDIAL CLASS

Setting

This experiment was carried out in the remedial department of a large modern comprehensive school (740 pupils from 11 to 16 years). Pupils selected for the remedial department spend about 50 per cent of their time working with teachers whom they know and trust. The subject was a rather small, under-weight boy of 13 whose work was well below that expected for his age. He was aware of his weaknesses and tended to display a number of avoidance strategies. He made a great deal of fuss before settling to work and took any opportunity to stop. He set himself up as a 'funny man' to gain attention and approval from his peer group. He became very anxious if asked to work alone (on the Language Master, for example), and would soon begin to interact with others, usually to their annoyance or detriment. His behaviour became disruptive if he encountered the slightest difficulty and if the teacher was not immediately available.

Method

The teacher allowed three weeks of the new term to pass, as a settling in period, before any attempt was made to collect baseline data. The operational definitions of behaviour for this purpose were:

(1) getting out of seat and moving two paces or more to touch another child's work; and
(2) unrequested verbalisations which can be heard over a distance of 2 metres.

A sampling technique was employed for observation so that the teacher could get on with her job of teaching for most of the time. A tape-cassette was played which gave an audible cue thirty times during a half-hour period but at variable intervals. The signal was loud enough for the teacher to hear but not loud enough to distract the class. Every time she heard the signal the teacher would look at Timothy and tally his behaviour as on-task or one of the categories of disruption, as defined above. On-task behaviour was defined as 'getting on with whatever he had been given to do'. Baseline data were collected on five successive days for thirty minutes during the time set aside for English, which occurred at a different period on each day.

The baseline records indicated that Timothy had been on-task for only a small percentage of the sampled times. He was very shocked when he saw a graphical representation of these data. He had not realised that he 'wasted so much time', as he put it and asked, 'What are *we* going to do about it?' Because of his obvious concern and his relative maturity it was decided that he should be involved in the monitoring of the intervention, by self-recording.

The intervention programme was aimed at increasing on-task behaviours by using the Premack principle, that is, increasing the incidence of a low-priority behaviour through the manipulation of a high-priority behaviour. Timothy was very fond of using a Doodle Art sketch-pad to colour in a cartoon picture and this was made contingent upon on-task behaviour. The boy was accordingly given the opportunity to tally his on-task behaviour using an observation schedule like his teacher's and the same signal. He knew that the teacher would be recording at the same time and understood that only those tally marks for on-task behaviour which were agreed between them would count. Ten such agreed tally marks could be exchanged for two minutes of the reinforcing activity, that is, colouring in the Doodle Art picture. At the end of the third week Timothy expressed dissatisfaction with this method of recording. He found having to stop working to tally his on-task behaviour a distraction. He was allowed to use a pocket counter instead.

During weeks seven and eight the teacher arranged a return to baseline conditions so that Timothy did not record his on-task behaviour and was not told his 'score' until the end of the week. He continued to earn time for the reinforcing activity, however. During weeks nine and ten, Timothy once again recorded his on-task behaviour every time the signal was heard.

Results

As can be seen from Figure 7.2, on-task behaviour during the baseline conditions was at a mean level of approximately 30 per cent. During the first intervention period it rose to over 70 per

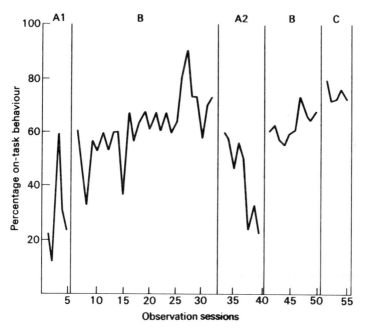

Figure 7.2 *Graph to show percentage on-task behaviour tallied for each (daily) observation session (teacher's scores).*

A1 – baseline   B – self-recording
A2 – reversal   C – follow-up checks (six weeks after)

cent with a mean of 62·3 per cent. For the two weeks when the boy ceased to record his own on-task behaviour this level fell to a mean of 40·3 per cent, rising again to a mean level of 61·0 per cent for the last two weeks. When the boy first began to record his own behaviour the level of agreement for the week between his results and those of his teacher was just over 90 per cent. After the first week the level of agreement never fell below 93 per cent and the mean level for the eight weeks was 96·5 per cent. This is very satisfactory.

The end of the programme coincided with the end of the term. The next term Timothy agreed to try to maintain his on-task behaviour without the aid of self-recording, although the teacher maintained her social reinforcement in response to his efforts. After six weeks she carried out baseline observations just as she had done at the beginning, using an ear-piece with the recorder so that Timothy would not be aware of what was going on. The graph (Figure 7.2) shows that there is good evidence that his rate of on-task behaviour was being maintained at a high level.

Discussion

This is a most interesting study for a number of reasons. It was very well controlled considering that the teacher was working entirely alone. It involved an older child, one who was aware of his problem and prepared to co-operate in seeking a solution. It depended upon operational pinpointing, a random schedule of observation sampling and produced good, objective data. The graph demonstrates clearly the measure of control obtained whilst there was good evidence of generalisation of effects, both subjective and objective. One of the chief effects of the intervention was that Timothy began to receive positive reinforcement for well-defined acceptable behaviour instead of for 'clowning' and other avoidance behaviours. This could be looked upon as the first stage on the way to his becoming subject to the natural, intermittent schedules of reinforcement which keep most of us in line with the expectations of our group.

It should be noted that whilst Timothy was improving his on-task score, the teacher was also manipulating the nature of the tasks being set. By degrees, she made the tasks more difficult in the sense that they tended to be those that Timothy found less to his taste and more likely to arouse his anxiety. These were mainly tasks which called for him to work alone and to solve his own problems and included individual exercises and work like SRA reading tasks. There was subjective evidence of generalisation to other situations and of a change of attitude within the boy. He showed greater self-reliance and his self-confidence was seen to increase. He began to express interest and increased keenness in the subjects he was hoping to follow in the next year when a degree of choice would be possible. It would seem that, in this case at least, 'teenage' children are not too sophisticated to respond to a simple intervention. It appealed to his peers as well as to Timothy himself.

The initial stages of setting up the operational definitions and observing may seem to be time-consuming for the teacher but once this has been done the actual intervention can be carried out without disruption of the teacher's routine. In this case the peer group were older children and could see for themselves the purpose and method employed. Thus any sense of mystery was avoided as was the possibility of jealousy from the extra attention that Timothy was getting. They all knew the problem and were just as keen to see Timothy settling down to his task and leaving them alone as was the teacher.

Chapter 8

Interventions with Groups or Classes of Children

In the previous chapter we reported demonstration studies describing interventions with individual children. The behavioural approach lends itself to dealing with the behaviour of groups of children equally well. Teachers will often experience classroom management difficulties as the result of one particular child's undesirable behaviour but more often than not problems arise from, perhaps less severe, but more generalised, misbehaviour on the part of the class as a whole. Indeed, in this book we have continually emphasised that a major concern is with the management of general classroom social behaviour. In this chapter we present a series of demonstration studies illustrating a variety of intervention techniques and methods of bringing about changes in the behaviour of groups or classes of children.

Like the demonstration studies concerned with individual children, those reported here vary in the degree of rigour displayed. Not all of the studies report numerical data, for example. It is not always possible, even if it is always desirable, to collect the quantity and quality of data one would ideally prefer whilst continuing to carry out general teaching activities. Nevertheless, the studies reported here which do not include much reference to data were judged to be successful by the teachers who undertook them and they provide a rich source of ideas for possible interventions which can be readily employed in most classrooms. We also include examples of more carefully controlled studies reporting appropriate numerical data, and references to further published sources are, as we have said, provided in the section headed 'Suggestions for Further Reading' at the end of this book.

CLASSROOM DEMONSTRATION STUDY 7

A SUCCESSFUL ATTEMPT TO REDUCE SWEARING AMONG NURSERY-AGE CHILDREN

Setting

This programme was set up in a nursery centre, administered jointly by the social services and education departments, which is housed in a Victorian infant school building in an inner city area. The children who attend come into contact with about twelve members of staff from time to time, since they work in shifts. The problem arose with a group of four children, two 3- and two 4-year-olds, who had developed a practice of walking around the centre together, swearing and chanting. All four had other behaviour problems but it was decided to concentrate on this particular behaviour as it was beginning to spread and some parents had complained.

Method

Observation over a week showed that swearing was more likely to occur at certain times than at others. It was shown to be most frequent during free-play time, that is, between 9.00 and 10.15 in the morning, immediately after dinner (between 12.30 and 1.30 p.m.), and again before group-time in the afternoon between 1.45 and 2.15 p.m. At other times these four children tended to be engaged in different groups and were not able to indulge in this sort of undesirable behaviour.

Once the observation had been completed the children were taken on one side and it was explained to them that swearing was unacceptable. They were then told that each one would be given a cardboard ladder to be placed alongside a tree that they had already made. The ladders would represent a day, each one being divided into three sections – before dinner, during dinner-time and after dinner. If they managed to pass the period without being heard to swear, a cut-out figure to represent each child would be moved up a step on the appropriate ladder. By this means a child successful in not swearing would be on the top rung at the end of the afternoon. The reward for this was to be allowed upstairs, a place normally reserved for the staff, where they were allowed to play with some special language equipment. The daily record of behaviour for each child was kept by a designated member of staff who was also responsible for taking them upstairs, if they were successful. It should be noted that the reward held the interest of the children since it was regarded as a rare privilege and was, at the same time, educational in outcome.

Results

Since each child was on an individual programme it is necessary to look at the results for each separately.

As can be seen from Table 8.1 this scheme worked perfectly with one of the children, Norman. After it had been working well for three weeks it was decided to set up a different model. This time a train was produced with a figure that could be moved along from carriage to carriage, each carriage representing a day. Three days of non-swearing would carry the child from the rear to the front carriage and earn the reward of going upstairs. After a further two weeks it proved possible to wean the child off this type of reward system and he took his train home. The swearing had stopped.

With another child, Tarik, and this was the one who had started the habit of swearing, there was a similar outcome, although there was one day when he lapsed completely. In this case the parents were also involved and they used a similar reward system at home. After three weeks he too was put on a 'train' programme and two weeks later this proved to be no longer necessary.

Table 8.1   *Results for Norman (Incidence of Swearing Behaviour)*

	Before dinner	During dinner	After dinner
Thursday	*	*	*
Friday	*	*	*
Monday	*	*	*
Tuesday	*	*	*
Wednesday	*	*	*
Thursday	*	*	*
Friday	*	*	*

* = success   − = failure

Table 8.2 *Results for Terry (Incidence of Swearing Behaviour)*

	Before dinner	During dinner	After dinner
Thursday	*	*	*
Friday	–	*	
Monday	–	*	*
Tuesday	–	–	*

* = success   – = failure

The third child, Terry, found the whole day too long a period and it was decided, therefore, to divide it into two sections only. He was allowed to go upstairs if he did not swear in the morning and again if he managed to refrain in the afternoon. This worked well and after a few more days the original strategy was reinstated with success.

With the fourth child, Graham, the system proved to be far less successful. This was due mainly to the fact that his attendance was very irregular. As a result, the reward system was not applied with any degree of continuity. The blame for this failure can, however, hardly be placed upon the programme. It is simply a fact that the programme was not applied because the child was not present.

Conclusion

The group of four no longer play together in their former disruptive manner and they certainly do not swear any more. Individually, their general behaviour has improved so there is some evidence of generalisation of effects. The teachers feel that the success of their intervention was dependent upon their choice of the reward which was very desirable for the children and thus proved to be very effective. Another point of interest was the evidence that was provided for the effectiveness of careful and selective pinpointing and observation. It enabled the teachers to vary their strategies as required and, finally, to phase out the intervention altogether. There is as yet no empirical evidence but it would appear to be self-evident that simple programmes, such as this, carried out at an early stage might prevent more serious behaviour problems from developing later on.

CLASSROOM DEMONSTRATION STUDY 8

AN ATTEMPT TO IMPROVE THE EATING BEHAVIOUR OF NURSERY SCHOOL CHILDREN

Setting

This study is concerned with the eating behaviour of young children attending nursery school. Several of them had learned poor eating habits which appeared to be very resistant to change. The nursery teacher involved found it a major problem to persuade some of her group of nursery-aged children to eat their school meals. Some children would eat virtually nothing and in many cases this appeared to be pandered to by their parents, that is, their 'finicky' eating behaviour was accepted and, indeed, reinforced by the lavish provision of sweets and crisps as alternatives between meals.

The subjects consisted of three girls and five boys aged 3 years 1 month to 4 years 6 months (mean 3:9·5) and comprised the lunch-time group regularly supervised by the nursery teacher. She was a female graduate (nursery trained) in her late twenties and in her second year of teaching. The children attended a social priority nursery school attached to a junior/infant school situated in an urban area with a high Asian and West Indian immigrant population. Typically the children arrive at 8.45 – 9.30 and are given a small rusk on arrival or shortly afterwards as a matter of nursery routine. No further food or drink is provided until lunch-time, which usually commences at midday. Children take their school meal in a family group of eight at a table supervised by a teacher or nursery nurse, who serves each child with food.

Method

The only materials involved were sheets upon which details were recorded for each child regarding how much of each constituent of the first (savoury) course of his school dinner he had consumed. Basically, constituent foodstuffs making up the meal were assigned to one of four categories: protein (meat, cheese, eggs, etc.), carbohydrates (bread, potatoes, pasta, etc.), green vegetables (peas, beans, cabbage, etc.) and non-green vegetables (swede, carrots, baked beans, etc.).

The teacher served a standard portion of each foodstuff to each child which was estimated at slightly less than that which the average child might eat, leaving sufficient over for second helpings for those who wanted it. Quantities obviously varied between foodstuffs but were fairly constant over time (for example, the cooks always provided roughly the same amount of mashed potato for eight children every time this was served), and the amount of foodstuff given to each child initially was approximately constant.

The teacher then rated for each child every day the amount of food in each category he had consumed on the following (self-explanatory) scale of increasing consumption:

0 = food in this category not even tasted
T = food tasted, but less than half of it consumed
M = more than half of the food in this category consumed, but not all of it
C = all food in this category consumed.

Data of this kind were collected daily under three different conditions, each phase lasting two weeks. The study lasted for eight weeks.

Under the first, *baseline* condition, the teacher merely served the food and did not comment at any point on eating behaviour. Dessert was non-contingent (that is, given regardless of whether they had completed their first course) and crisps and other edibles (which the children had brought in with them) were freely available at the afternoon break when milk was served.

Under the second, *contingent praise* condition, a 'rules, praise and ignoring' strategy was employed. The following three simple positively phrased rules were formulated and announced daily at the beginning of lunch-time:

(1) We try to get on with our meals quietly.
(2) We try to taste everything on our plates.
(3) We try to eat up all of our dinner.

Infractions of these rules were ignored; no verbal punishment or other comments were made. Children abiding by these rules were liberally praised in terms such as 'Look how well Anthony is getting on with his dinner', 'Good girl, Stella, you've tasted your cabbage', 'I see Gareth has eaten up all of his dinner – that's very good'. Again provision of dessert and afternoon break edibles was non-contingent.

Under the third, *contingent dessert* condition, the procedure was similar to contingent praise except that dessert and edibles at afternoon break were given *contingently* upon improvement in the individual child's eating behaviour. Children were told that only if they ate more than they usually did would they obtain dessert and afternoon snacks. (Afternoon snacks were made available to all children 'qualifying' even if they had not brought any sweets or crisps with them, by the use of left-over dessert or by a judicious redistribution of wealth!) Improvement was determined by the teacher and was thus necessarily, in part, subjectively based but children were continually and individually informed of the expected target behaviour: for example, 'Now Gareth, I want you to taste everything today and then you can have your pudding'.

Following the contingent dessert phase, a return was made to the praise condition for a further two weeks in an attempt to determine the effect of whether withdrawal of contingent dessert would lead to a drop in appropriate eating behaviour or whether it would now be maintained by praise alone.

Results

The baseline data showed that four children almost invariably consumed all of almost everything given to them. Ninety-two per cent of all portions were fully consumed on average (range 89·5 – 94 per cent) and 100 per cent of everything was at least tasted in each case. Moreover, this pattern continued over the succeeding experimental phases and consequently we will not dwell further on these children.

The other four children, however, showed low-level and variable eating behaviour during the baseline phase. On average, only 18·5 per cent of all portions were fully consumed (range 9·5 – 34 per cent) almost all of which were carbohydrate or protein portions. Looking at overall figures, Table 8.3 details overall percentage consumption figures for the four categories of food over the four conditions averaged for these four children.

For carbohydrates the most important area for improvement was in eating more or finishing, since the vast majority of carbohydrate portions were at least tasted. Contingent praise served to raise the level of both eating more and finishing (consuming all) food in this category by over 20 per cent. Contingent dessert appeared to exert little additional effect. A similar overall picture emerged for protein where eating most and

Table 8.3 *Percentage Portions of Food in Each Category Fully Consumed (C), Consumed or Mostly Consumed (M) and At Least Tasted (T) over the Four Experimental Conditions Averaged for the Sub-Group of Four Children Identified as Poor Eaters*

		Conditions			
		A	B1	C	B2
Carbohydrate	T	95	97	100	100
	M	68	84	85	76
	C	47	66	67	69
Protein	T	76	78	79	90
	M	40	50	61	55
	C	26	38	42	48
Non-green vegetables	T	58	44	76	72
	M	11	19	36	41
	C	00	9	15	17
Green vegetables	T	50	28	68	58
	M	10	22	37	17
	C	3	13	5	17

A – baseline   B1 – contingent praise
C – contingent dessert   B2 – contingent praise

finishing were again primarily increased by contingent praise. In the case of vegetables, however, both green and non-green, the more powerful reinforcer of contingent dessert and afternoon snacks was necessary to improve tasting and consumption appreciably. Tasting actually went down for the first praise condition, but, in the main, the second praise condition served to maintain gains made by contingent dessert.

We may compare the (estimated) percentages of food in each category consumed by the four poor eaters featured in this study, both during baseline and during a period of two weeks' observation undertaken four months after the completion of the study. (It should be noted that the contingent dessert strategy was subsequently maintained for this group of children after the completion of the study.) We believe that these figures speak for themselves (see Table 8.4).

Table 8.4   *Percentage of Foodstuffs Eaten before and after the Intervention*

	Carbohydrate	Protein	Vegetables non-green	green
Baseline	70%	46%	23%	21%
Post-study	100%	81%	75%	70%

Comments

A reasonable degree of success may be claimed for this study, in so far as the four children whose eating behaviour was identified as low level and erratic have been shown to be consuming more food in all categories overall. Moreover, it was shown that particularly troublesome eating behaviours, such as eating or even tasting/sampling vegetables, are often responsive to strategies employing the contingent provision of dessert and afternoon snacks. It was also shown that a rules, praise and ignoring strategy will sometimes have an effect and that for some children it is a preferable technique. We should, however, immediately stress that it would be foolish to imagine that these are the only, or even the major, influences on eating behaviour even within the context of this study. The food varied randomly over conditions as did the general health and well-being of the individual children.

CLASSROOM DEMONSTRATION STUDY 9

ENCOURAGING TIDINESS IN A RECEPTION CLASSROOM

Setting

The teacher found that when the children, aged 4 to 5 years old, were playing with toys like 'Lego' or 'stickle-bricks' or when using apparatus like 'Unifix', beads for threading, or shapes for sorting, the floor became littered with dropped pieces. Accordingly, a great deal of time was wasted clearing up at the end of the session. She felt that apart from the time-wasting there was another issue, namely, the need to teach children to be aware of objects that had been dropped and the necessity of retrieving them, there and then, before they were damaged or lost.

Method

The teacher had two groups of between eighteen and twenty children coming to her at separate times for certain sessions. These she designated red and green groups. She explained to the children that at the end of each five minutes of the twenty-minute session a timer would sound. (A kitchen timer was used for this purpose.) If the floor, at that time, was clear of pieces the group would receive a green (or red) star to be stuck on a chart which was prominently displayed on the wall. Each group could thus earn four stars in a session.

Results

The effects were immediate. On most occasions when the timer sounded the teacher looked at the floor and found it to be clear. After five sessions the stars were totalled as shown in Table 8.5. Each child was given a 'smartie' for trying whilst the members of the green group had an additional 'smartie' for having most stars.

Comments

The result was time saved in clearing up, a successful attempt to keep the floor tidy and a lesson in awareness and responsibility. This intervention was soundly based from the behavioural point of view since the task was clearly within the competence of these young children whilst the reward system allowed for no 'losers' – a very important point, especially with such young children. The stars were easy for the teacher to handle and were displayed on a chart that was clearly visible so that the children could see what progress they were making. Note that the task objectives were made realistic in that quite short periods of time were involved, children of this age not being able to cope with a long time scale.

Table 8.5 *Token Chart for a Reception Class*

Sessions	1 2 3 4	1 2 3 4	1 2 3 4	1 2 3 4	1 2 3 4	Totals
Red group	* * * –	– * – *	– * * *	* – * –	* * * –	13
Green group	– * * –	* – – *	* * * *	* * * –	* * – *	14

CLASSROOM DEMONSTRATION STUDY 10

USING TEACHER TOUCH EFFECTIVELY IN THE INFANT CLASSROOM

Setting

This study was concerned with the effect of contingent touch upon disruptive behaviour and the on-task behaviour of infant class children. It was carried out in a two-form entry primary school in an Educational Priority Area in the West Midlands. Sixty-five per cent of the children in the school are from immigrant backgrounds (mostly Asian) and this proportion was reflected in the two classes chosen. Observations were carried out in two classrooms in which the seating was arranged informally around six to eight pairs of tables.

Two female teachers and their respective classes (classes 1 and 2) took part. The first teacher, aged 45, a graduate with a postgraduate teaching certificate, had nineteen years' experience and had been in the school for the previous four years. There were twenty-eight children in her class, sixteen boys and twelve girls. The second, aged 49, was a non-graduate, two-year-trained teacher who had completed five years' teaching at the school and had previously worked part-time or on supply teaching in various schools. Of the twenty-eight children in her class, sixteen were boys and twelve were girls. Both teachers estimated that over half of the children in their respective classes entered school speaking very little English, with about a third who knew hardly any English words.

Method

Each class and its teacher was observed for ten sessions, each of twenty-seven minutes' duration, for the collection of baseline data using a classroom observation schedule. This schedule was designed to sample teacher behaviour and children's rates for disruption and on-task behaviour. Four sessions out of each series of ten were observed by a second observer using an identical observation schedule sheet in order to calculate inter-observer agreement. For the purposes of observation touch was defined as, 'The teachers' hand or part of the hand and/or arm to be in contact with the child's body'.

At the conclusion of the baseline sessions the planned intervention procedure was put into effect. The teachers were asked to touch the children every time they praised them but not at any other time. It was emphasised that no deliberate increase of praise was required; the rate of praising was to be kept as before, as far as possible. The teachers were given no details about the observation schedule but were again observed, as before, for a further ten sessions. Once again, four of these sessions were used to obtain information on inter-observer agreement.

Results

The inter-observer agreement figures varied between 80 and 100 per cent, with an average of 89 per cent which is very acceptable. Mean percentage on-task behaviour rose appreciably for both classes, as the graphs in Figure 8.1 show. Class 1 improved from an average of 78 per cent to 95 per cent whilst scores for class 2 rose from an average of 72 per cent to 90 per cent. Similarly, disruptive behaviour was much reduced in both classes following the intervention. As the graphs in Figure 8.2 show, disruptions fell from an average of 9·5 to 3·2 in class 1 and from 11·6 to 2·4 in class 2. The amount of non-contingent touch by the teachers in both classes was much reduced but total teacher touching remained about the same. In other words, both teachers successfully followed the instructions to touch only contingently and neither to increase nor decrease their overall use of touch. Although a reversal was not attempted, this study appears to show that this simple strategy of restricting the use of touching for reinforcement only is an effective way of improving the classroom behaviour of young children.

Comments

This is a simple, non-intrusive technique for teachers to employ but its uses are limited, probably to the younger age range. Teachers would hardly be advised to use it with adolescents, say, particularly of the opposite sex!

A reversal would have been preferable in order to 'prove' the effectiveness of the technique scientifically but this was not possible, as is often the case in research in the real world. Teachers are understandably reluctant to abandon a technique they are finding useful merely to prove a point for researchers. One

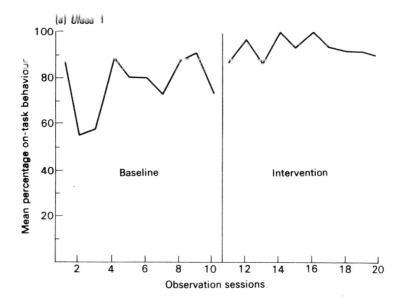

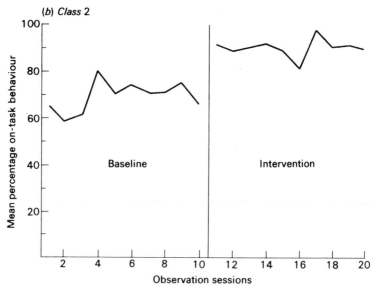

Figure 8.1   *Mean on-task behaviour per session:*
    (a)   Class 1
    (b)   Class 2

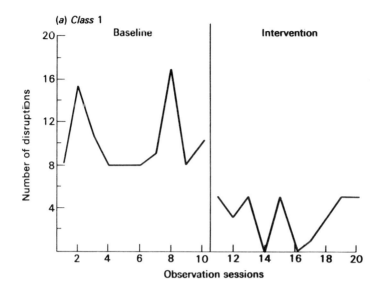

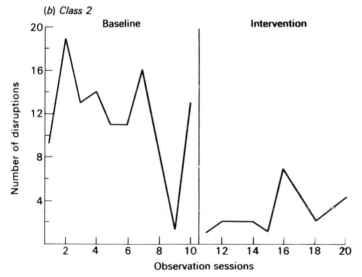

Figure 8.2   *Total number of disruptions per session:*
    (a)   Class 1
    (b)   Class 2

criticism that can be dismissed, however, is that the changes were due to overall increases in the amount of praise used. The data showed clearly that praise rates remained about the same before and after the intervention.

CLASSROOM DEMONSTRATION STUDY 11

SCHEMES TO GET CHILDREN TO REMEMBER SIMPLE ROUTINES

Setting

These interventions were carried out with two groups of younger boys and girls in a junior school by two teachers each working with her own class. Neither class was particularly difficult to handle. These were simply small routine matters which cause teachers' nerves to fray and can lead to a great deal of negative 'nagging' behaviour on the teacher's part.

Method

(1)   The pencil rally   The aim of this was to get all the children to remember their pencils for both morning and afternoon sessions. The teacher provided a large sheet of paper with a race-track drawn on it. This was pinned up on the wall so that everyone could see it. She also provided a number of large pictures of cars that could be fixed on to the track with 'Blu-tack'. At the beginning of each session the teacher asked the children to show their pencils. If everyone in the class had his or her pencil then one car was put on the track. To begin with, as soon as there were five cars on the track every child received a sweet. Later, ten cars were necessary to earn the same reward. The same basic idea was applied by the teacher to the bringing of reading-books to the classroom. In this case, however, instead of checking at the beginning of the lesson she would make her check at random times when the children were unprepared.

(2)   The PE ladder   Many of the children from this class seemed to forget their PE clothing. The teacher devised a PE ladder, which was a chart placed on the wall in the form of a ladder. There were

eight steps, one for each letter of the phrase 'PE ladder'. Each of these letters was covered by a piece of paper held in place by 'Blu-tack'. Every time all the class remembered their PE kit the teacher removed one of the pieces of paper, disclosing the letter underneath. When all eight letters had been uncovered the reward was a 'free' PE lesson in which the children were allowed to choose the activities. This proved to be a very popular reward which the children were prepared to strive for, showing once again that the simplest schemes can be very effective with children when teachers are imaginative.

(3)   Remember your book   This intervention was also carried out by the second teacher. The children at this school were encouraged to take their reading-books home but some were not very good about bringing them back again the next morning. Two or three children, on average, every day from this class would forget to bring their books. In order to solve this problem the teacher took a sheet of wrapping-paper which had a complete picture on one side of it. This she cut into five unequal and irregular polygons. Each morning a check was made and if all the children had brought their books back a child was allowed to paste up one part of the picture on to a framework. When the picture was complete with all five pieces in position the children enjoyed a reward, usually a sweet each.

Results

In each of these cases there was an immediate improvement in the number of children remembering their pencils, their PE equipment, or their reading-books. There was not a 100 per cent response, of course, but as we suggested in Part One, we are not trying to produce saints. In the case of the third study, for example, on only one or two occasions per week would a child fail to come to school with his book. This was a great improvement and a situation that was much easier to cope with.

Comments

These three simple devices show how effective use can be made of the behavioural approach by imaginative teachers and with little expenditure of effort. They also show how children tend to respond to the approach. Each has the same basic features:

(a)   a clearly defined behaviour to be observed and counted;
(b)   a clear visual record for the children; and
(c)   a clear and effective reward.

CLASSROOM DEMONSTRATION STUDY 12

INCREASING ON-TASK BEHAVIOUR IN A JUNIOR CLASS

Setting

These interventions were carried out by the teacher of a group of twenty-nine 7- to 8-year-olds in a junior school. The teacher felt that some children were not concentrating sufficiently on their work. They spent a lot of their time chatting, playing around and generally distracting those seated nearby.

Method

An attempt was made to increase on-task behaviour and, hence, the output of work. The procedure was explained to the children just as they were about to begin working individually at a set exercise. During the lesson the teacher moved around the classroom correcting work, and so on. As she did so she was observing the children carefully, and any child seen to be getting on particularly well or doing good work was praised and allowed to go to the front of the class in order to place a coloured bead in a dish placed there for the purpose. If the teacher observed a child who was not getting on, he/she was required to place a black bead in another, separate dish. The game was generally played for about thirty minutes at a time when a balance would be struck between the contents of the two dishes.

In another situation the teacher used groups into which the children were already organised for working as the basis for a game. The teacher would be sitting in front of the class and hearing children read to her. The children were told that she would be looking from time to time to observe the groups and that she would tally her record if all the members of the group were working. Times for looking up and the order for the groups to be looked at were not controlled. The teacher reports that before the experiment she looked up more often than not to tell a child to stop talking or to get on with his work, to sit down, or something similar. When this game was in operation she looked up and commented only when a group had succeeded in doing something that she had asked them to do.

Results

In both cases the result was an increase in the incidence of on-task behaviour and an improvement in the amount of written work produced when compared with that achieved in similar sessions before the experiments. The teacher reports that many of the children surprised themselves by the amount of work they produced; instead of a few lines they now managed to complete the whole of the set exercise in the given time. She also felt that the giving of praise improved the children's confidence and thus caused them to try harder the next time. However, the teacher found that having the children come to the front of the class in the first game to place their beads tended to be disruptive, so at a later stage she placed the beads in the dishes herself and this proved to be a great improvement.

Discussion

Both these interventions are examples of consciously applied strategies which cause the teacher to pay attention to good behaviour and (largely) to ignore unwanted acts. The results are as behavioural teachers would expect. Both these games would have been improved if some more objective definition of working and good behaviour had been given. This is where some positive rules would have been useful so that the positive reinforcement given could then have been related to a specific rule.

CLASSROOM DEMONSTRATION STUDY 13

IMPROVING ON-TASK BEHAVIOUR IN A CLASS OF
7- TO 9-YEAR-OLDS

Setting

This study was carried out in a primary school in the West Midlands with a catchment area including both private and council houses, with the majority of children coming from lower socio-economic class backgrounds. The subjects consisted of a class of 7- to 9-year-olds and their teacher. The mixed class included fifteen 7- to 8-year-olds and eight 8- to 9-year-olds. The class teacher, a female graduate with five years' experience, had no major problems regarding class control but had found the class difficult at the start of the year.

Method

The teacher regarded talking out of turn and general chatting and 'out of seat' behaviour as the main difficulties she was experiencing. Consequently it was decided to focus on on-task behaviour and on her own teaching behaviour.

Using a specially designed observation schedule, the children's on-task behaviour was observed and recorded by an observer for three minutes and then teacher behaviour was observed for a further two minutes. The observation periods were thirty minutes long and consequently each cycle of on-task and teacher behaviour observation (five minutes in total) was repeated six times. In order to satisfy the criterion for on-task behaviour each child had to be paying attention to the assigned task for the full four seconds during which he was individually observed. Attention to the assigned task would include writing or recording without looking up, listening or responding to the teacher and legitimate movement around the room. Each child was individually observed in this way once per observation cycle and the total number of children 'on-task' recorded. Observation of teacher behaviour included the recording of all positive and negative responses to both social and academic behaviour by the teacher. Baseline data were collected in this way for three half-hour sessions on different days.

Following the collection of baseline data an intervention strategy was initiated. The intervention was based on the game strategy employed in demonstration study 16. Materials included a cassette tape-recording of a bell which rang six times in each thirty-minute session on a variable interval, on average every five minutes. A list of three positively phrased classroom rules was put up on the wall of the classroom following discussion with the class. The rules were as follows:

(1) We get on quietly with our work when children are standing at the teacher's desk.

(2) When our work is finished we find our next job quietly.
(3) We only get up out of our seats when the teacher calls us or when we need to ask for help.

When the behavioural game was in progress the cassette-recorder would be switched on and every time the bell sounded the teacher would look at one of the four tables at which the children were seated. If all members of the team on that table were following the rules they would be awarded a point in the form of a coloured (unifix) cube. Each team had the same number of turns overall, but in a random sequence. The cubes signifying the points earned were made clearly visible and the teacher used verbal praise to back up the giving of the points.

Three further observation sessions were conducted when the game was in progress.

Results

Mean on-task behaviour during baseline was around 57 per cent. This rose to a mean of just over 91 per cent following the intervention (see Figure 8.3). The results for teacher behaviour

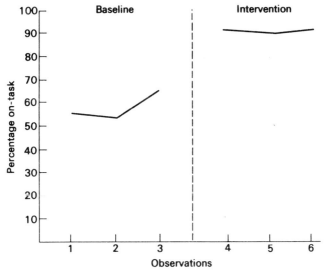

Figure 8.3 *Percentage of on-task behaviour before and after the implementation of the 'game' strategy.*

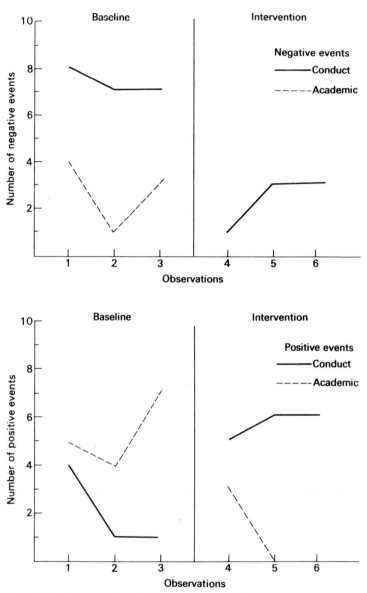

Figure 8.4   *Teacher behaviour before and after the implementation of the 'game' strategy.*

are shown in graph form in Figure 8.4. Negative teacher responses to both social and academic behaviour dropped markedly whilst a clear increase in positive responses to social behaviour was in evidence. Positive responses to academic behaviour, however, declined.

Comments

The results provide a clear demonstration of the effective use of a behavioural game strategy in classroom management. On-task behaviour improved considerably and the 'timer game' cued the teacher to respond positively to appropriate social behaviour and to refrain from negative responses to both academic and social behaviour. The decline in positive responses to academic behaviour is difficult to explain but a contributing factor may have been that the teacher employed a much quieter voice during the intervention sessions which made it difficult to hear all of her comments to individual children at her desk.

It is important to point out that the teacher spontaneously made several other changes to her classroom procedure. These included putting extra work up on the board for children who finished quickly and telling children at the beginning of the lesson exactly what to do on the completion of their first task. She also checked to see that every child had a sharp pencil and that there was an eraser on every table. It could be argued that these constitute changes in the antecedent events for academic behaviour and hence any changes in on-task behaviour may, at least in part, have been attributable to these changes.

Teacher praise for social behaviour only occurred when cued by the bell during the timer game. The teacher subsequently indicated that she found it difficult to use praise more naturally. Similar difficulties were experienced by the teacher in demonstration study 16.

The children's enjoyment of this device was obvious and on several occasions they were observed to be 'policing' the game by putting their fingers to their lips to quieten individuals who might be breaking the rules. They also spoke in quieter voices when approaching the teacher and waited until they reached her desk before they spoke to her. A major disappointment, however, linked to the teacher's manifest inability to generalise her praise, was that the children quickly returned to their 'normal' noisy out of seat behaviour once the game was over. In other words, the teacher failed to generalise the new behaviour to situations other than the game.

CLASSROOM DEMONSTRATION STUDY 14

ENCOURAGING A JUNIOR CLASS OF CHILDREN TO MOVE ABOUT THE SCHOOL QUIETLY

Setting

This intervention was carried out by the teacher of a group of thirty-three children of mixed ability aged 9 to 10. The problem was that they made a lot of noise when moving about the school. This included coming in from the playground at the beginning of sessions and moving from the classroom to the hall and back for PE. The teacher believed that part of the problem lay in the antecedent conditions. When coming in from the playground the children were required to make two lines, one for boys and one for girls. This meant that two very long lines were formed in which the children tended to jostle each other to be first or last. The corridor from the playground to the classroom is very long, as is that from the classroom to the hall. In addition, there are two corners to be negotiated and a set of fire doors. This means that it is impossible for the teacher to keep an eye on all the children as they move about the school. If the teacher stayed behind, the children in front would race ahead, whilst if she led the file, children at the back lagged behind and became noisy. Most of the other classes in the school behaved in much the same way but being smaller did not appear to create so much confusion.

Method

School policy required that children should learn to go about the school quietly but the teacher had enjoyed no success in changing the behaviour pattern by using traditional means, that is, shouting at the children or making them all come back to carry out the manoeuvre again. She decided, therefore, to change the antecedent conditions. The children were given instructions to form three lines in future. There were thus only eleven children in each and they were given set positions in the line so that there would be no pushing for places in future. Particularly noisy children were separated from each other, three being appointed to act as line leaders. The leaders were given strategic stopping places, for example at the corners, so that the teacher could control the movement more easily. After reorganisation of the lines the whole exercise was made into a game, to show that this was the best class in the school. The class were reading a book called 'A dog and a half' at this time and the teacher suggested that the class should call itself 'A class and a half'. From this point on the teacher indicated approval by using social reinforcement in terms of encouraging words and gestures as each stopping-point was reached without noise or fuss. This change in behaviour was noted by the class next door and the friendly rivalry which this engendered between the two groups was encouraged by both teachers.

Results

This strategy proved to be extremely effective. Other teachers commented quite spontaneously on the 'quiet class coming up the corridor' and when their previous teacher made such a comment it was particularly rewarding for the children. The giving of social reinforcement was continued for some time and every so often treats of one sort or another were contrived when the children did well.

Gradually, the reinforcement was reduced to the occasional 'Well done' or a reminder just before the class left the room. Now the class moves quietly and at a moderate pace about the school and classes other than the one next door are beginning to follow suit.

Comments

We see here how the teacher used a change in the antecedent conditions together with social reinforcement very skilfully to bring about desired behaviour change. At the same time she managed to use competition in a way that caused no harm to any individual. Perhaps of even greater significance is the way she managed to achieve a high degree of generalisation so that the behaviour is now being maintained by naturally occurring contingencies.

CLASSROOM DEMONSTRATION STUDY 15

CHANGING PRIMARY SCHOOL CHILDREN'S ON-TASK BEHAVIOUR BY CHANGING THE SEATING ARRANGEMENT

Setting

Two parallel studies comparing 'tables' and 'rows' type seating arrangements were carried out in two junior schools. In each school a fourth-year class of 10- to 11-year-old children was chosen. One class consisted of twenty-eight boys and girls of mixed ability attending a school in an urban residential area, whereas the other class consisted of twenty-five similar children from a school on a council housing estate. In both classes the children normally sat around tables in groups of four, five and six, except for end-of-term tests when they sat in rows. The design, procedure and results of the two studies were very similar.

Method

The children were initially observed for two weeks (ten days) in their normal seating arrangements around tables. An observation schedule using a time sampling procedure (described below) was employed to obtain estimates of on-task behaviour. This was defined, by the teachers, as doing what the teacher instructed, that is, looking at and listening to her when she was talking to them, looking at their boxes or work-cards when they were required to complete set work, being out of seat only with the teacher's permission, and so on. In the second study observations were carried out at different times and included all lessons except PE, art and music, whereas in the first study observations were made only during purely academic lessons when the children had been given specific work to complete. Calling out, talking to neighbours, interrupting, and so on, were regarded as off-task by the observers in both studies.

The observation schedule required each child to be observed twice per lesson in random order for thirty seconds. This was broken down into six five-second periods. If the child was on-task for the whole five seconds he scored one point; if off-task for any part of the five seconds he did not score. Hence, this yielded a score of six for each thirty-second period and a score out of twelve for the two observation periods per child per lesson combined, which was subsequently converted to a percentage. This gave us an estimate of percentage on-task behaviour for each child for each lesson which, when averaged, gave an estimate of on-task behaviour for the whole class.

After the class had been observed for two weeks sitting around tables (baseline data), the desks/tables were moved into rows without comment from the teacher and the children were observed for a further two weeks of observation (eight days in the first study; ten days in the second study). Finally, the desks were returned to their original positions, again without comment, for a further two weeks of observation (seven days in the first study; ten days in the second study). This time there were a few complaints from the children since they said that they *preferred* sitting in rows.

Results

Mean on-task behaviour for both classes was higher when the children were placed in rows than when they were seated around tables. Mean on-task behaviour in class 1 was 72 per cent under 'Tables 1', 88 per cent under 'Rows' and 69 per cent under 'Tables 2'. Similarly for class 2, mean on-task behaviour was 67 per cent under 'Tables 1', 84 per cent under 'Rows' and 72 per cent under 'Tables 2'.

Looking at individual children, the most marked improvements in on-task behaviour occurred with those children whose on-task behaviour was previously very low. As we might expect, the effect was less in the case of children with high initial on-task behaviour. One or two children in each study showed *higher* on-task behaviour in tables – especially one child in the second study, the noisy ring-leader of an anti-school group, who spent most of his time in rows trying to regain contact with his group!

Comments

As the graphs in Figure 8.5 show, control over children's on-task behaviour by the manipulation of seating arrangements (that is, antecedents) is clearly possible, especially with children whose initial on-task behaviour is low. Using antecedents in this, or other, ways may prove to be a more immediate means of gaining control over some children's classroom behaviour. This may also prove a useful bridge whilst other behavioural teaching skills are learned

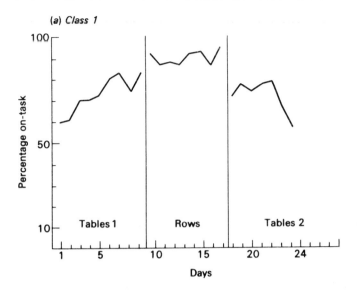

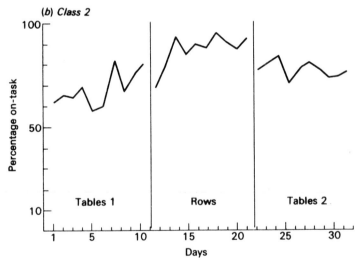

Figure 8.5 *Average on-task behaviour for the two classes over the three phases:*
(a) *Class 1*
(b) *Class 2*

and could serve to increase instances of desired behaviour for the teacher to reinforce.

Why does classroom seating around tables lead to more off-task behaviour whilst seating in rows leads to improved on-task behaviour? The tables based seating arrangement is, quite simply, geared towards enhancing social interaction. It facilitates eye contact, a prime means of initiating a social encounter, and provides a setting for increased participation in such interactions by involving the whole group. After all, we engineer such seating arrangements in precisely this way when we wish to encourage social interaction, in committees or when playing bridge, for example. Moreover, tables provide ideal cover for covert aggression or teasing by means of kicking or pinching under the table, thereby increasing disruption. Rows formations, on the other hand, minimise both forms of social contact, allowing fewer occasions for the teacher to comment adversely and more instances of desirable behaviour for him or her to comment upon favourably. In short, it would be argued that it amounts to little short of cruelty to place children in manifestly social contexts and then to expect them to work independently.

It must immediately be emphasised, however, that a return to rows for all work is *not* being advocated. It is offered only as a possible strategy to encourage academic work which requires the child to concentrate on the specific task in hand without distractions. Rows would be totally inappropriate, for example, for small group discussions or group topic work, where table arrangements might prove more effective. These are empirical issues which have to be tackled in future research.

CLASSROOM DEMONSTRATION STUDY 16

A 'GAME' APPROACH TO INCREASE ON-TASK BEHAVIOUR IN A JUNIOR SCHOOL CLASS

Setting

The primary school in which this study was carried out was situated in the centre of a large council housing estate in the West Midlands. The teacher was a young, relatively inexperienced woman who had just completed her probationary year successfully. However, in her own estimation she was having a lot of trouble in controlling her class of thirty intellectually below-average 10- to 11-year-olds. Classroom seating was arranged around four groups of tables and it was decided to make use of this very common arrangement in the intervention strategy.

Method

A cassette-tape was prepared to give a clear 'ping' on a 'variable interval' schedule of sixty seconds, that is, the signal occurred at irregular intervals but on average once per minute. On hearing the sound the teacher would look at one of the four tables of children, indicated in random order on a prepared sheet, and note the behaviour of the target child for that table by ticking the appropriate column. The target child was chosen afresh for each observation session on a random basis and thus all children in the class were observed during the study. Every time she heard the 'ping' the teacher had to glance at the schedule to see which table was next and record the behaviour of the target child by ticking the appropriate code. She could do this whilst working at her desk and, with experience, whilst walking around the room still advising individuals and commenting on their work. The reliability of the teacher's results was checked from time to time by an observer using an identical record-sheet and the same target children. There was found to be very high inter-observer agreement of around 90 per cent.

After several weeks of practice, 'baseline' data were collected, that is, data collected prior to the teacher being given any instruction in behavioural methods. By averaging over sessions it was calculated that the children were on-task, that is, quietly getting on with their work, for only 44 per cent of the time. The teacher was then given some basic instruction in the behavioural approach, which was entirely new to her, and was helped to choose an intervention which appealed to her and which she felt she could cope with.

The children were told the rules of a 'game', which were:

(1)   We stay in our seats whilst working.
(2)   We get on quietly with our work.
(3)   We try not to interrupt.

These rules were to be clearly displayed in the classroom. Whilst the game was in progress, the cassette tape-recorder would be switched on and every time the 'ping' sounded the teacher would look at one of the tables. If everyone on the table was keeping the rules, then each child on the table would score a house point. (They were assured that all tables would get equal turns but that the order would be random.) Each time a team point was given it was announced publicly and accompanied by verbal praise. This procedure lasted for five weeks when an amendment was announced. In future points would be awarded on only 50 per cent of the signals, again on a random basis. The 'pings' continued to serve the teacher as a signal for observing and recording the behaviour of the target children as well as a signal for reinforcement.

Results

The results were remarkable and immediate and are shown in graph form in Figure 8.6. From the baseline average of only 44 per cent, on-task behaviour rose to 77 per cent following the intervention. Moreover, when the amendment to the schedule of reinforcement was made, after five weeks, the on-task behaviour rose even higher to between 80 and 100 per cent. Interestingly the *quality* of off-task behaviour also changed. Whereas before the intervention, disruptiveness was mainly shown in loud talking and quite a lot of movement around the room, afterwards, off-task behaviour consisted mainly of passive inattention, day-dreaming, watching other children, and so on.

A purely subjective estimate of the classroom after the intervention was of great improvement in terms of orderliness and quiet during classroom work periods. An attempt was also made to measure academic output both before and after intervention. Samples of written work taken from the class during the collection of baseline data showed a mean output of approximately five written words per minute. During one of the first intervention sessions this had improved to a mean of approximately thirteen written words. However, the number of spelling errors, despite the big increase in output, had hardly changed.

Comments

The teacher used the term 'harrowing' to describe her problems with class control in her previous (probationary) year. She found that the recording of baseline data proved 'tedious and

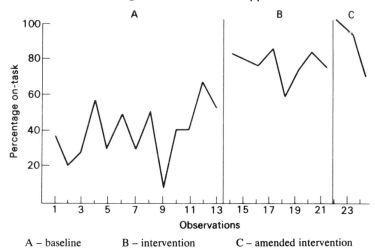

A – baseline   B – intervention   C – amended intervention

Figure 8.6   *Graph to show on-task behaviour observed by the class teacher as a percentage of all responses observed.*

time-consuming' at first but she thought that it became easier and less distracting after practice. She agreed that the effect of the intervention was immediate and very positive and said that she would continue using behavioural techniques especially to provide positive reinforcement for good behaviour. The reactions of the children were very positive and several commented upon the fact that the quietness that prevailed enabled them to concentrate and get on with their work without interruption.

It had initially been supposed that some stronger back-up reinforcement might be needed to make the game effective, but the house points proved to be sufficient on their own. This may sound an elaborate intervention to set up but, in fact, is not so. A signal can easily be put on to an audio-cassette and any machine used to play back. Observing and recording have to be mastered but teachers improve quickly with practice. This device has been seen to work effectively with many age-groups and in many situations. The great problem is one of generalisation which calls for skilful use of social reinforcement while the game is in operation and a careful phasing out of the use of the 'game' itself.

CLASSROOM DEMONSTRATION STUDY 17

A 'RULES, PRAISE AND IGNORING' PROJECT WITH A
GROUP OF 11- to 12-YEAR-OLDS

Setting

The children were in the top age-group of a middle school. The
teacher was young and lively and was providing many good
learning experiences for her group of twenty children. They were
well-behaved on the whole and produced work of good quality.
Despite these conditions the teacher decided that some aspects of
classroom management could be improved and to this end she
suggested setting up some rules for the classroom to improve the
change-over from one lesson to another.

Method

The teacher asked the class to write down their ideas for suitable
classroom rules. After discussion a consensus was reached as to the
three most popular ones. As might well have been expected, two
of them were in the form of prohibitions. The teacher explained
that it would be better if the rules were expressed in more positive
terms and that they needed to be clear and definite in intention.
The rules which were eventually agreed and displayed prominently
in the classroom were as follows:

(1) Please put your hand up before speaking.
(2) Please be prepared for the next lesson within three minutes.
(3) Please remove any unwanted objects from your table.

It was then agreed that if the children were keeping the rules
they would receive a point. Points were given for rule 1 at any
time; rule 2 operated at the end of each lesson, and rule 3 when
each lesson began. Monitors were appointed to mark up the scores
– one each for girls and boys. A wall-chart was displayed so that
the score could be seen clearly by everyone. It was further agreed
and promised by the teacher that all children who achieved the
target of eight points set for the week would be able to take part in
an extra period of games. In subsequent weeks the target was
raised.

Results

Only one child failed to achieve the target during the first week and to receive the reward of extra games. For the second week the target was raised to ten points and this time all the children managed to reach it. In subsequent weeks the target was raised still further and children who did not reach it were debarred from the extra games period. They had to spend the time on academic work under the supervision of another teacher. It is interesting to note that the girls' scores were generally lower than those for the boys at the outset but they increased steadily. The boys' scores started generally higher and were maintained, except for the last week. These results are shown in the form of a graph in Figure 8.7.

Comments

The teacher felt that the programme had an immediate practical effect in improving the children's adherence to the rules they had agreed upon. The maintenance and improvement of the scores

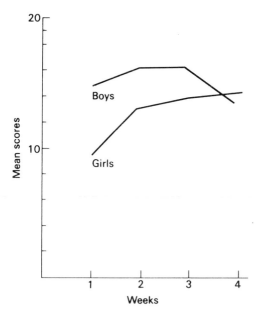

Figure 8.7   *Graph to show points scored by girls and boys*

also reflects this. However, she found that the project 'ran out of steam' by the third week and she had to work hard to inject some enthusiasm to keep it going. It was, to be true, the end of the school year. She felt that had it not been so near to the end of the term she would have explored other means of bringing about and maintaining behaviour change. Nevertheless, she felt that it had been a very interesting and useful experiment.

CLASSROOM DEMONSTRATION STUDY 18

INCREASING THE RATE OF ORAL RESPONSE IN A MIDDLE SCHOOL FRENCH CLASS

Setting

This intervention was carried out by a male teacher with a group of 12-year-olds in a middle school in the West Midlands. The children were drawn from different classes and met four times a week for French lessons. They constituted the 'middle set' of the year group and the course followed was 'En Avant'. Generally, the children did not show great enthusiasm for their French lessons and did not respond well in oral sessions, most of the responses coming from fewer than a quarter of the group. Since willingness to respond in oral work is essential to the success of the course the teacher decided to use a behavioural strategy in order to increase the rate of responding of the members of the group.

Method

In order to obtain a baseline the teacher began to tally the number of responses per lesson given by the children in a normal week. Once this had been done he explained the scheme to the class. They were told that every time a child made a correct response to a question in French or English, as appropriate, he or she would receive a plastic disc. The teacher was to be the sole judge as to the correctness or otherwise of the response. The target was for every child in the group to earn one counter per lesson or an average of one per lesson over three lessons. If the target was achieved, then during the fourth lesson of the week the children would be allowed to illustrate the booklets which they were writing in French, something which they liked doing.

Results

The graph of the results in Figure 8.8 shows clearly that the intervention had an immediate and lasting effect. The mean level of responding at baseline was 1·05 and after the intervention began it was 1·76, an increase of 66 per cent.

Comments

There were a number of practical problems. The teacher found it physically exhausting and time-wasting to move around the classroom to give out the counters. It would have been better had he found some other way of tallying the children's responses or of letting them do this for themselves. He tried to raise the rate of responding to two per pupil per lesson at a fairly early stage and this proved to be too much, mainly because the lessons were relatively short. Some children became upset if they were unable to meet the target set and this is something that behavioural interventions should avoid at all costs.

One boy who had been very keen to answer before the

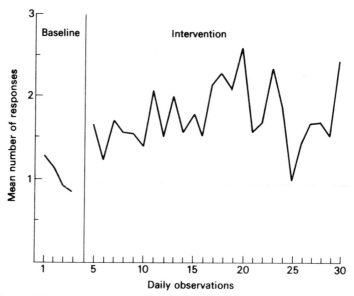

Figure 8.8 *Graph to show rate of responding in French lessons.*

intervention started complained that he was given far fewer chances to answer afterwards. This, of course, is an inevitable consequence of more involvement of the rest of the class. This is an interesting study because few have been attempted with subjects like modern languages. It helps to support the contention that the behavioural approach has wide application.

CLASSROOM DEMONSTRATION STUDY 19

IMPROVING STUDY BEHAVIOUR IN A SECONDARY REMEDIAL CLASS

Setting

This programme was set up in a large comprehensive school in the West Midlands. The subjects were a class of eight girls and eight boys who had been placed in a remedial group after the administration of a battery of standardised tests. The mean age of the group was 12·7 years and their mean reading age, as measured by the Schonell Silent B test, was 9·5 years.

The general feeling of the staff was that the class members were too noisy, that they did not get down to work quickly enough and that when they did, their work output was below what it should have been. The teacher approached the class about these issues with which they showed general agreement and they agreed also that an intervention should be set up.

Method

A simple recording sheet was provided for each child for the week (see Table 8.6). For the whole of one session per day (it was always an English lesson) a tape was played which emitted an audible signal on variable interval schedule of sixty seconds. The signal thus occurred thirty times during the half-hour session but with a variable period between each sound of from fifteen to ninety-five seconds. To the class it would appear to sound at irregular and unpredictable intervals. The children were told that if they were working, that is, concentrating upon whatever task had been set, when the signal occurred they could make a tally mark in the appropriate line. The marks were totalled at the end of the session and at the end of the week. The teacher hoped to be

Table 8.6 *Recording Schedule for On-Task Behaviour*

Date	30-minute session (English)	Totals
Monday		
Tuesday		
Wednesday		
Thursday		
Friday		
	Weekly total	

able to regard this first week's score as a baseline but it can be seen from the records (Figure 8.9) that scoring was high from the start. From the outset the 'ping' became a highly discriminative stimulus for getting on with work. Since they never knew when it would sound next, the only way to be sure of being able to mark a tally was to work constantly. Scores for the first week averaged 133·5. The teacher used the lowest score of all (86) as a guide for setting the target for week 2. Accordingly she set this target at 80 as being realisable and promised a reward. This reward was a thirty-minute session on Friday afternoon in which all children who met the target could follow activities of their own choosing. The weekly target was raised by small steps to 120 for the fifth week.

The teacher asserts that since the children sat in small groups around tables they could easily check up on each other when marking the tallies and that the incidence of cheating was low. The teacher herself was also able to keep a check on cheating because the children knew that she could oversee them whilst they were marking their tallies on the sheet.

Results

In spite of the gradually increased target score only one child ever failed to reach the target set. The results are summarised in Figure 8.9 in the form of a graph. Subjective evaluation of the effects of the intervention made by the class teacher and other members of the staff suggested a considerable improvement in noise levels.

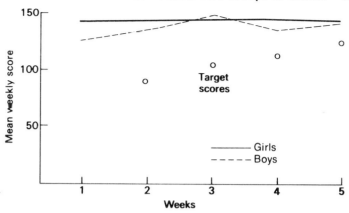

Figure 8.9 *Graph to show mean scores for on-task behaviour (self-recorded).*

The amount and the standard of work completed had also greatly improved. The Christmas holiday brought a natural break in the experiment and the class agreed to try to maintain both behaviour and work levels without the help of the signal. Although this was not entirely successful there was general agreement among the staff concerned that some of the improvement in work and behaviour was maintained into the new term.

Since the products of the present experiment were in written form it was possible to take a measure of a more objective kind. Samples of work done by members of the group during a thirty-five-minute English lesson both before and at the end of the intervention were available and from these, two measures were obtained. A crude, but objective, measure of quantity was obtained through a word count, whilst a more subjective measure of quality was obtained by having a teacher-colleague award marks for neatness and presentation. The teacher/marker awarded these marks 'blind', that is, without knowing which set of papers related to which stage of the intervention nor of the purpose of the evaluation. This was an attempt to avoid bias.

Table 8.7 shows that the number of words produced and the marks for neatness both improved for boys and girls. These findings support the subjective evaluation of the teachers reported in the paragraph above and give credence to their opinion about the improvement in work output.

Table 8.7   *Mean Scores for Work in English Lessons*

		Before intervention	At end of intervention
Boys:	Neatness scores	5·57	6·71
	Word count scores	132·57	178·86
Girls:	Neatness scores	6·38	7·25
	Word count scores	129·88	199·00

Comments

Apart from the interesting data showing the effects of a behavioural intervention aimed at social behaviour upon work output, there are a number of other important issues that arise from this study. To begin with it is interesting to note that these children accepted the intervention as reasonable and were able to carry out the self-recording effectively and conscientiously. The effects of the intervention were felt immediately, the signal becoming an antecedent event which influenced behaviour from the start. The high scores which were made at the outset were maintained throughout. The raising of the target score could have been manipulated more effectively, however, in view of the high initial performance. Nevertheless, the intervention was clearly successful and did not cost the teacher an unreasonable amount of effort.

CLASSROOM DEMONSTRATION STUDY 20

INCREASING ON-TASK BEHAVIOUR IN A SECONDARY MATHS LESSON

Setting

This study was undertaken in a large, split-site, multicultural, co-educational comprehensive school with a group of twenty-five academically below-average 14- to 15-year-old boys and girls during their maths periods. They were being taught by the headmaster of the school. The class gave trouble to most teachers who attempted to teach them and even the head admitted that they could be troublesome.

Initial observations showed the headteacher to be highly skilled. He had established a good working relationship with the children. He used praise fairly frequently and rarely raised his voice.

Method

Baseline data were collected over eleven lessons in which on-task behaviour was observed and recorded. All twenty-five children were observed for at least two thirty-second periods during each lesson in random order. The amount of time within each thirty-second period spent by the child in on-task behaviour was recorded on a cumulative timer-stopwatch. The results for the two (or more) thirty-second sessions per lesson were then summated and percentage on-task behaviour per child per lesson thereby estimated. A second observer was also present on six occasions during the baseline and subsequent phases to provide estimates of inter-observer agreement which were consistently over 90 per cent. Despite skilful teaching the class was on-task for only just over half the time.

The observations indicated that a large proportion of the off-task behaviour occurred when some of the class (the quicker ones) had finished the task set for them, usually consisting of a number of examples written up on the blackboard. It was at this time chiefly that they would indulge in off-task behaviours themselves and disrupt the work of others. It was suggested to the teacher that he should manipulate antecedents for on-task behaviour by putting up extra problems on the blackboard for the quicker children to get on with until all the class had finished the basic set. Following this first intervention, observation continued for a further seven sessions.

It was decided that on-task behaviour could be improved still more and a multi-element or alternating conditions design was agreed upon. On the first, and thereafter on every other day, a simple 'rules, praise and ignore' strategy was employed. The rules for this were:

(1) When the teacher is talking to us we look at him.
(2) We get on with our work quietly.
(3) We try not to stop others from working.
(4) We try to pay attention to our work and try not to daydream.

These were printed on card, read out at the beginning of every lesson and also, on occasion, referred to during the lesson but *not* contingent upon infractions of the rules. Infringements of the rules were to be *ignored* unless serious or dangerous disruptions occurred. On the other hand, the teacher was instructed to look out continually for pupils keeping the rules, individually or collectively, and emphatically praise those pupils: for example, 'It's good to see Errol, David and Patrick getting on with their work'; 'Susan is working well'; 'This is good, I can see you are all working well'.

In addition to this, on the alternate days, a 'timer game' was introduced where points for on-task behaviour were awarded. Basically a cassette was played which emitted a chime on a variable interval averaging two minutes. The chimes were a signal to the teacher to look up to see if the class were observing the rules. (This was partly a subjective estimate on his part but it was felt that a simple yes/no decision procedure like this was preferable to a more complicated observational sampling procedure which many teachers find off-putting.) If they were all observing the rules (in his view) he awarded a point and praised the class. Each point was worth one minute's free time during the last maths lesson of the week on Friday afternoon. Scoring twenty-five points would win the whole lesson off. (The Friday lesson was prone to interruptions for judo club and other activities and hence was not used to collect data during this study. Consequently it proved an ideal 'free' lesson for use as a reinforcer.) During the free period the children could chat quietly but freely (a surprisingly uncommon opportunity for many children in secondary schools) or play games such as draughts or cards which were supplied. This multi-element design was implemented and observations continued for a further fifteen lessons.

Results

The average percentage on-task behaviour for the class during the baseline phase was fairly stable over the eleven lessons at around 55 per cent (varying between 43 and 63 per cent). After the extra sums were put up on the blackboard average on-task behaviour rose by nearly 15 per cent to an average of 69 per cent. The multi-element design clearly showed the relative effectiveness of the two subsequent procedures which improved on-task behaviour still further. On the 'odd' days when the 'rules, praise and ignore' strategy alone was employed, on-task behaviour rose to over 80 per cent, overlaid by improvement by yet another 10 per cent to over 90 per cent on-task behaviour (on average) on 'even' days when the 'timer game' was played. It should be noted, however, that after twelve lessons the rates for the two conditions merged at around 95 per cent average on-task behaviour. This is shown clearly in Figure 8.10.

Discussion

This is powerful evidence for the success of behavioural procedures in secondary school classroom management. Moreover, the study shows that significant improvements in on-task behaviour may be achieved using only 'light' behavioural technology such as the manipulating of setting events ('more sums') or simple 'rules, praise and ignoring' strategies. It was especially gratifying to see that overt praise was so effective with adolescents within their peer group.

The headmaster, after over twenty-five years of teaching, found extreme difficulty at first in consistently using praise contingent upon good conduct and ignoring minor infringements of the 'rules'. However, ultimately this change in his behaviour resulted in the maintenance of on-task behaviour in the 80–90 per cent range. A point of contention might be use of 'free time' as a reinforcer. In this study it was the opinion of the headteacher that in the four lessons per week under behavioural control, sufficiently more progress was made in comparison to pre-intervention lessons to justify 'free time' as a reinforcer. That is, more work was done in the four lessons than in the five lessons previously.

CONCLUDING COMMENTS

The final two chapters of this book reporting demonstration studies have brought together, in real-life examples, what we have learned about the general theoretical model underlying the behavioural approach to teaching, the accompanying methodology which allows us to analyse problem behaviours and the technology with which we can attempt to deal with these behaviours in the form of specific interventions. We have attempted to show that teachers can dramatically improve their teaching performance and achieve superior classroom discipline by careful study of the behavioural approach and the learning of appropriate behavioural skills and techniques.

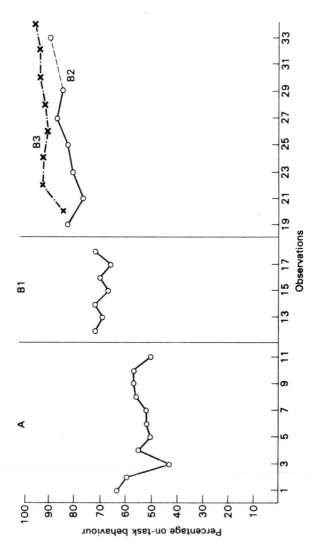

Figure 8.10 *Percentage on-task behaviour of the class during the experiment.*

A – baseline   B2 – 'rules, praise and ignore' intervention
B1 – 'antecedent' intervention   B3 – 'timer game' intervention

As we have maintained from the outset, teaching is concerned with the business of deliberately changing children's behaviour. Teachers are paid to do just that. The behavioural approach is, to our knowledge, the first and only approach which not only faces up squarely to this fact but also provides a carefully validated and scientific means of achieving it. We hope that by this stage we have shown clearly that the behavioural approach is not only soundly based but is also, by its very nature, practical and practicable. It provides a continual stream of ideas for teachers working at the 'chalk face'.

It has sometimes been suggested that the theoretical model may be new, but that the techniques have long been known and are already widely employed. To this we would reply that it is true that the behavioural approach to teaching systematises and brings together a variety of effective teaching techniques, most, if not all, of which have already been discovered. There is a world of difference, however, between a rag-bag of hit and miss procedures (employed with no thorough understanding of how or why such techniques do or do not work in certain circumstances), and a structured and integrated model such as that employed by the behavioural approach.

Moreover, we would go on to say that it is not the case that behavioural techniques (perhaps under a different guise) are already used widely in schools. Indeed, we are tempted to add that if they were, far fewer problems would be in evidence. To take a simple example, our own research shows that teachers' use of approval and disapproval in dealing with social behaviour is almost totally at odds with what the behavioural approach would advocate. Teachers praise children very infrequently for appropriate social behaviour whilst disapproving continually of the children's inappropriate behaviour. (Nor do we see much evidence for publicly displayed, let alone positively phrased, classroom rules and seating arrangements.) The behavioural approach is much more subtle than simply attempting to be Mr Nice Guy (or Ms Nice Gal) in the classroom. It is *not* about continually beaming your approbation of anything and everything children in your class may do. It *is* about recognising children's appropriate behaviour and providing consequences for it which they will find reinforcing and according to a carefully predetermined system. Few of us are able to do this naturally. It is something that we have to work at. We have to learn new skills and techniques which it is unlikely that we shall have encountered either in our initial training or on in-service courses. But they are well worth learning since the behavioural approach offers the brightest hope for improved classroom management, a less stressful teaching experience and a happier classroom for pupils and teacher.

Suggested Answers and Possible Solutions to Exercises

CHAPTER 2

Exercise 1

Statements *b*, *e* and *h* are all consistent with the behavioural approach. The rest are not.

(*a*) Whilst we might accept that certain temperamental differences are inherited, nevertheless we would regard 'being able to concentrate' as learned behaviour.

(*c*) Almost all behaviour is learned and particular behaviour can only be judged in its social context. Consequently, bad behaviour is just as much the result of learning as good behaviour.

(*d*) Children develop 'naturally' by responding to the reinforcing and punishing events in their environments. It is these contingencies which bring about changes in behaviour.

(*f*) This is a pessimistic prognosis with which the behavioural approach has no sympathy. All human behaviour can be changed although with some people it will be a slow process and we may not be able to teach them as much as others.

(*g*) An attitude is nothing more than a disposition to behave in a certain way. In fact, the only way by which we can judge a person's 'true' attitude to a situation is to observe his behaviour in the face of it. Behavioural teachers freely acknowledge that their task is to change children's behaviour and, consequently, their attitudes and values.

Exercise 2

Statements *a*, *c*, *f*, *g* and *h* are all 'explanatory fictions'. The causes they refer to are merely other ways of describing the same behaviour. The other statements are behavioural explanations because they refer to independent factors (in these cases, consequences) which control the behaviours.

CHAPTER 3

Exercise 1

Case (a) *Not getting on with work* Probably the easiest way would be to pinpoint his writing behaviour by counting the number of figures or words Gerald writes in each working session. This would be entirely objective and later on, in an intervention, would be a measure which is clear to him and, equally clearly, under his control. Alternatively, you could pinpoint on-task behaviour. Maybe he is not on-task long enough to produce satisfactory quantities of output. On-task behaviour could be defined as 'looking at his book/paper, the blackboard, or at the teacher'. Again, you could look at in-seat behaviour. Perhaps he is finding all sorts of reasons for being out of his seat. For this purpose we would need a definition such as 'in-seat means that the child's bottom is on his own seat and that the seat is in its proper position, that is, facing the right way and with all four legs on the ground'.

Case (b) *Talking* In the case of Tracey the pinpoint is fairly obvious. Since she hardly ever speaks a simple count of all her utterances should be quite an easy way of pinpointing her verbal behaviour. With George, however, we need to establish some sort of criterion and this will probably have to be whether the teacher can hear him or not. The pinpointed behaviour will then become each occasion on which the teacher can identify his voice above the general noise of the classroom.

Case (c) *Attention-seeking* For Mary you will perhaps need to pinpoint two behaviours. For calling out behaviour it could be 'anything called out to you by way of an answer or in order to attract your attention for which you had not given permission'. For the other behaviour you would have to count the number of occasions when she left her seat to talk to you without being given permission.
These are not the only acceptable answers. The acid test is whether the pinpoints you have chosen can be easily identified and whether they constitute clear actions on the part of the children which can be observed and counted.

Exercise 2

Definitions *b*, *c*, *e*, *f* and *h* are all easy to observe and count. In item *f* minding his own business is difficult to define but it is also redundant. If he is getting on with his work then he must be minding his own business. All the other definitions are too vague. Making a fuss, being untidy, bullying, and so on, could be interpreted in different ways by different people or even by the same people at different times and so would be quite useless for pinpointing.

Exercise 3

At first sight she seems to have some good data here. We can see clear differences between one day and the next and between morning and afternoon counts, but when we begin to look for explanations the weaknesses emerge. We have to ask:

(a) What is her definition of bad behaviour? How do we know that she always uses the same criterion? Note the importance of pinpointing and writing out the exact definition on the schedule. Up to now you may have felt that this was being too careful.

(b) For what period is she observing? All the time? In which case, how can she teach at the same time or, alternatively, how can she watch whilst she is helping a particular child? Probably she just looks up from time to time and this may be when an extra lot of disturbance is going on. Note the importance of having some pre-planned time for observing or having a cue.

(c) Were her children so much better on Monday? Or did she alter her criterion as the week went on? Why were they so good on Friday afternoon? Perhaps they really were or maybe she was preoccupied with the coming weekend or too harassed to notice or perhaps, by then, she just forgot.

(d) Since we have no indication of the length of the period for which observations were made we cannot calculate rates of responding and, therefore, graphical representation would be misleading. On Wednesday afternoon she might have been watching for twice as long as on Friday.

(e) She is committing the cardinal error, for a behavioural teacher, of equating naughty behaviour with naughty children. As behavioural teachers we have to judge behaviour in a particular situation and in relation to its rules. Children will respond to the settings and contingencies which teachers provide. If these are wrong the resultant behaviour may well be maladaptive but the children should not then be described as naughty. This is labelling and leads us to *expect* certain behaviours.

CHAPTER 4

Exercise 2

In the following table we have attempted to set out remarks suitable for reinforcing particular behaviours with different age-groups.

Behaviour	*Young children*	*Junior children*	*Secondary children*
Quietness	That's lovely, Jane. You're working as quietly as a little mouse.	Well done, 3R. I could have heard a pin drop. You've been so quiet.	This is fine, 4H. When it's quiet like this we can all get on with our work.
Politeness and co-operation	I hope you all noticed what a polite boy Graham was when he wanted me to help him.	Roger, I really liked the way you were so willing to share your book with Paul.	Thanks, Pamela, it makes my day when someone goes out of her way to lend a hand (for example, when collecting in exercise-books).
Answering appropriately	That's super! I saw at least ten hands go up without a sound.	That's the way, Jenny. You put your hand up then without shouting out.	That's a good point, Simon. I hadn't thought of that at all.
On-task behaviour	Just look at Diana and Charles, children. Aren't they working well?	Much better, 2F. I can see that everyone's hard at work.	Marion, I want you to know that I've noticed how hard you've been working (said privately).

Exercise 3

Among other activities you could try are these:

For the class		*For the individual*	
(*a*)	Free time	(*a*)	Caring for classroom animals
(*b*)	Choice of activity	(*b*)	Acting as monitor
(*c*)	Extra PE or games or other lessons	(*c*)	Tidying up the cupboards
(*d*)	Visit or trip out of school	(*d*)	Taking work to the headteacher
(*e*)	Going out early	(*e*)	Choosing the story to be read or other activity to be done.

CHAPTER 5

Exercise 1

There are, as usual, a number of answers in a situation like this, all of which could prove to be effective. In Part Two of this book (classroom demonstration study 14) you can read for yourself how one primary teacher tackled this problem in an imaginative way and with great success.

Exercise 2

Here we have to deal with a behaviour (speaking out loud in class) which is completely lacking and for which we have observed a zero baseline of responding. We have, therefore, to teach the response (not from scratch, because the child can speak), of speaking publicly. He will speak privately to us as the teacher, given encouragement, so we have to decide how far down the left-hand column of the flow-chart to go and work upward from there. Perhaps to begin with we can encourage his responding in a small group or we can relay his privately given answers to the class. If he can get reinforcement from seeing his answer or contribution approved of by teacher and peers, perhaps he can be helped, by degrees, to give it for himself more and more often.

Exercise 3

This behaviour is plainly one that has to be eliminated or, at least, reduced. We have daily baseline data and probably the best approach would be to divide up the day into appropriate sessions, perhaps just an hour or so to start with. We could then arrange some rewarding consequence for sessions in which there is no reported hitting, pushing, jeering, mocking, or similar behaviour on the part of the subject. Tokens could be used to mark sessions in which success is observed and some back-up activity or other reward could be provided. This would also allow response cost to be applied if it was thought to be appropriate.

RECAPITULATION EXERCISES FOR PART ONE

Exercise A

(*a*) Explanatory fictions include hyperactivity and lack of 'inner control'.

(*b*) Since Mr Green has been telling him off constantly for being out of his seat this may have been a *reinforcing* event for the boy or, at the very least, a neutral event. Remember that whether an event is punishing or not can only be decided empirically, by its effect on behaviour.

(*c*) Pinpointed behaviours could be some objective definition of out of seat behaviour. It might be better, however, to look more positively for a definition of in-seat or on-task behaviour, which could then be increased.

(*d*) The chief problem is one of changing the consequences which have been maintaining the behaviour. This could be the teacher's comments or, perhaps, the consequences provided by his classmates. If the teacher now begins to provide some means of providing positively reinforcing consequences for remaining in-seat and getting on with his work, John's behaviour will be seen to change. The crucial issue for the teacher is to pick upon some reinforcer that John will 'go for'.

Exercise B

If you have read and understood the contents of the book, most of the 'correct' answers should stand out clearly. Remember that we were asking for 'the completion phrase which was most in line with the behavioural approach', and whilst the alternatives may not be exactly wrong we have indicated below the response which adheres most closely to the behavioural perspective. Where necessary we have added an elucidatory comment:

1	(*c*)	6	(*c*) or (*d*)	11	(*c*)	16	(*d*)
2	(*d*)	7	(*c*)	12	(*c*)	17	(*c*)
3	(*b*)	8	(*a*)	13	(*c*)	18	(*a*)
4	(*a*)	9	(*c*)	14	(*a*)	19	(*d*)
5	(*c*)	10	(*d*)	15	(*b*)	20	(*d*)

Comments

4. Alternative *a* must be our overriding concern at all times but this is not to deny the importance of parents' feelings or the emphasis on positive methods.

5. Not all troublesome behaviour is attention-seeking or, at least, seeking attention from you. Ignoring troublesome behaviour which is being maintained by peer attention will have no effect.

6. This is a trick question. Either *c* or *d* is likely to do the job. Which you use will depend upon the given circumstances.

12. In order to avoid disappointment it is important to remember that ignoring attention-seeking behaviour does often lead initially to more frequent troublesome behaviour before it declines.

13. Alternative *c* is the best option and is an example of an advanced technique known as backward chaining.

18. It is interesting to note that a contract, of course, is also a form of setting event in much the same way as are overt classroom rules.

19. Group contingencies have been shown to be a very good way of countering unwanted group reinforcement.

CHAPTER 6

Exercise 1

This teacher had indicated her timing and method with precision but her definition could be tightened up. For example, suppose that Harry goes

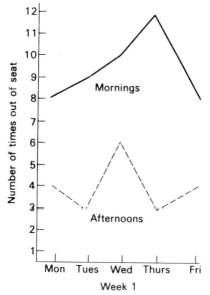

Figure E.1   *Graph to show Harry's out-of-seat behaviour.*

across the room and sits chatting to his friend. According to her definition he is sitting down and presumably would not be scored, yet he is not in his seat and is probably stopping other people from getting on. Again, he might shuffle his seat along, whilst still sitting on it, to get near his friend, thereby causing a lot of disturbance and yet not be out of his seat according to the definition. We need a definition like the one given earlier, viz., the child's bottom is to be in contact with his *own* seat and that has to be in its proper place and facing in the proper direction, otherwise 'out of seat' is scored. Apart from this she has collected good data. Since the time spent in observing is always the same she could plot her scores directly on to a graph because they are directly comparable. She would probably do best to keep morning and afternoon scores separate so the graph would look something like Figure E.1.

She might begin to look around for an explanation of the big differences between morning and afternoon scores. It could lie in the nature of the work. Perhaps Harry is more interested in the things that go on in the afternoon and therefore stays in his place more and gets on with his work, or it could be that in the afternoon at 2 p.m. he is tired out after rushing about in the playground after lunch.

Exercise 2

Number of agreed observations = 7

Number of disagreements   = 1

Inter-observer agreement $= \dfrac{7 \times 100}{7 + 1} = 87 \cdot 5\%$

This would be an acceptable level of agreement.

Exercise 3

For observation points 1 and 2 we have agreement on 5 and 4 respectively, as the number of children on-task. For observation point 3 you have 4 and the student 5, so here we would score agreement on four with one disagreement. Scoring in this fashion we get:

Number of agreements =
    5 + 4 + 4 + 3 + 5 + 5 + 2 + 4 + 4 + 4 + 3 + 5 + 4 + 4 + 5 = 61

Number of disagreements = 1 + 1 + 1 + 1 + 1 + 1 + 1 = 7

Inter-observer agreement $= \dfrac{61 \times 100}{61 + 7} = \dfrac{6100}{68} = 89 \cdot 7$ per cent.

This, again, would be a satisfactory result.

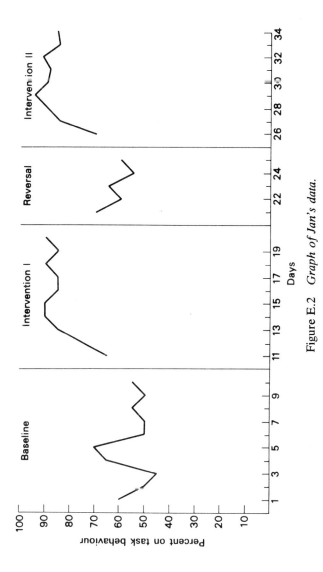

Figure E.2 Graph of Jan's data.

Exercise 4

Mean level for first 10 days $= 550 \div 10 = 55$
Mean level for 10 days of intervention $= 840 \div 10 = 84$
Mean level for 5 days of 'reversal' $= 310 \div 5 = 62$
Mean level for reinstatement (9 days) $= 783 \div 9 = 87$

The graph of on-task behaviour demonstrates that the 'rules, praise and ignoring' regime was very effective in controlling behaviour. As soon as it came into operation its effects were felt immediately and when it was temporarily abandoned on-task behaviour fell at once, almost to baseline level. As soon as it was reinstated the level of on-task behaviour rose once again to a very acceptable rate.

Suggestions for Further Reading

Fontana, D. (ed.) (1984), *Behaviourism and Learning in Education*, Monograph of the British Journal of Educational Psychology (Edinburgh: Scottish Academic Press in association with the British Psychological Society).
A British book of essays on the various ways in which behavioural psychology is applied in education. It includes a chapter by the present authors which refers to their development of the Behavioural Approach to Teaching Package or BATPACK – a structured, skills-based, in-service training programme for teachers held in schools.

Glynn, E. L. (1983), 'Building an effective teaching environment', in K. Wheldall and R. Riding (eds), *Psychological Aspects of Learning and Teaching* (London: Croom Helm).
An interesting chapter demonstrating the use of behavioural methods to improve *academic* performance in the classroom.

Merrett, F. E. (1981), 'Studies in behaviour modification in British educational settings', *Educational Psychology*, vol. 1, no. 1, pp. 13–38.
This paper provides a comprehensive review of intervention studies carried out with individual children and whole classes in this country.

O'Leary, K. D., and O'Leary, S. G. (1977), *Classroom Management: The Successful Use of Behaviour Modification*, 2nd edn (New York: Pergamon).
A first-rate collection of studies including some of the classic pioneering work carried out in the United States.

Vargas, J. S. (1977), *Behavioural Psychology for Teachers* (New York: Harper & Row).
A lively and practical introduction to the use of behavioural methods in the classroom. One of the best American texts but some aspects will appear strange to British teachers.

Wheldall, K. (ed.) (1981), *The Behaviourist in the Classroom: Aspects of Applied Behavioural Analysis in British Educational Contexts* (Birmingham: Educational Review Publications).
This book is, to our knowledge, the only collection of papers reporting work carried out in this country on the behavioural approach to teaching. It includes an extensive bibliography.

Wheldall, K. (ed.) (1982), *Behavioural Pedagogy: Towards a Behavioural Science of Teaching*, *Educational Psychology*, vol. 2, nos 3 and 4 (special double issue).

The journal *Educational Psychology* regularly publishes reports of behavioural work in the classroom. This special double issue includes papers by some of the international authorities in the field.

ASSOCIATION FOR BEHAVIOURAL APPROACHES WITH CHILDREN

This Association, in which the authors are heavily involved, exists to promote the use of behavioural methods with children. It publishes a quarterly journal, *Behavioural Approaches with Children*, which reports many studies carried out by teachers. It also offers a 'troubleshooting' service through which teachers with classroom problems can consult a panel of experts.

Index